ONTOLOGY
Milton's COSMOGONY
and PHYSICS

Walter Clyde Curry

Milton's

Published by the

ONTOLOGY

COSMOGONY

and PHYSICS

UNIVERSITY OF KENTUCKY PRESS

*Publication of this book
is possible partly because of a grant
from the Margaret Voorhies Haggin Trust Fund
established in memory of her husband
James Ben Ali Haggin*

To Kathryn, Josephine, and Ray

PREFACE

An expression of my appreciation is due to the editors of the North Carolina *Studies in Philology,* the *Journal of English and Germanic Philology, Anglia, Philological Quarterly,* and to the directors of the Vanderbilt University Press and the Stanford University Press for their very courteous leave to reprint here, with some revision and corrections, the subject matter of, respectively, Chapters I, II, IV, VI, III, and VII. I am also greatly indebted to the kindness of the following publishers: namely, to Houghton Mifflin Company for the privilege of quoting and basing arguments upon *The Complete Poetical Works of John Milton,* edited by Harris Francis Fletcher; to Burns, Oates & Washbourne for the right to quote and base arguments upon St. Thomas Aquinas' *Summa Theologica* as it appears in the authoritative translation prepared by Fathers of the English Dominican Province; to The Clarendon Press for the privilege of quoting extensively from C. R. S. Harris' *Duns Scotus;* and to the director of The Soncino Press for permission to use as indicated in the Appendix a translation of *The Zohar* made by Maurice Simon and Harry Sperling. Without the gracious cooperation of these and other publishers, editors, and scholars, the appearance of this book must have been measurably delayed.

I take especial pleasure in acknowledging the invaluable critical and bibliographical aid given me by Professors William B. Hunter of Wofford College and Robert Hunter West of the University of Georgia. I am also deeply indebted to Professor David A. Ruffin of Southern Methodist University for his very artistic adaptation of my original crude designs of the diagrams.

CONTENTS

CONFESSIONS
OF THE AUTHOR

DR. SAMUEL JOHNSON SAYS: "PARADISE LOST IS ONE OF THE books which the reader admires and lays down, and forgets to take it up again. None ever wishes it longer than it is. Its perusal is a duty rather than a pleasure. We read Milton for instruction, return harassed and overburdened, and look elsewhere for recreation. We desert our master, and seek for companions." During my twenty years of perusal, I, too, have often laid the work aside with confusion of mind, sometimes with embarrassment or frustration. But being impelled by an irresistible fascination, I have, unlike Dr. Johnson, returned as often to the poem, discovering with each successive examination new excellences of expression, new grandeurs of concept and organization, glowing symbols perhaps of truth, and inexhaustible sources of myth and legend woven into epic adventure. I have been privileged to travel much in the universes of all space—Heaven of Heavens, the Cosmos, chaos, and Hell—and have become partially acquainted with the Creator and with many of his interrelated creatures. Such travel in unaccustomed realms, even without any attempt to fathom the inner meaning of things, is not unaccompanied by harassment. The human mind becomes uncomfortable when required to expand beyond its normal, limited capacity; the imagination is likely to flag with weariness when it is constantly confronted by infinity and the almost immense. But the experience in itself is rewarding. (Acquiring knowledge concerning the origin and construction of the greatest of stages and superficial acquaintance with its company of titanic actors would seem to be the first step in the process of grasping the grand drama which Milton presents in *Paradise Lost*.)

I

Leaving Adam and Eve to their human activities, I have many times wandered through the vast expanses of the Mundane Universe enclosed in its stationary shell. Here one may look with wonder upon stars and planets dispensing light with mystic influence upon the tiny home of Man and rolling in courses prescribed by unalterable law centering in the Sun. Here Divinity can be pleased—and the chaste human spirit touched—by music of the spheres. I have watched with Uriel the awe-inspiring spectacle of this World's founding in chaotic darkness and its quick genesis into brilliantly lighted order; I have listened with reverence to Raphael's spirited account of its creation in six days. And being amazed, I have thought with Chaucer, "O God, much is thy might and thy noblesse." Passing the planets and fixed stars, one arrives at the marvellous crystalline sphere, the clear hyaline or glassy sea of circumfluous waters on which the Cosmos is built. I have often in imagination been wafted by angels over its jasper-green waves or rapt in a chariot drawn by fiery steeds over its flowing liquid pearl and deposited at the very foot of stairs, mysteriously meant, leading up to the west gate of Heaven of Heavens.

But here cross winds have often swept me to the backside of the World into what is now called the Paradise of Fools. In this Limbo of idiots and all things vain I have been distressed to discover placed my old mediaeval friends, the gentle St. Francis and the devout St. Dominic, together with their followers and their brothers the White Friars. These souls are human and therefore companionable, perhaps imperfect, but they have faithfully served humanity and God. It is also pitiful to see those pilgrims who, with spiritual zeal, sought Christ at the place of his death for them now roaming these windy plains with the unaccomplished works of Nature's hand. Surely such as these cannot suffer destruction at the "final dissolution" forecast?

But when the mystic stairs are lowered, permission is often granted me, an earthly guest, to enter the majestic western gate of Heaven, to travel the noblest of highways leading through a heavenly landscape, and to arrive in mid-Heaven before the awe-inspiring throne of God himself as he sits clothed and concealed in ineffable Light forever. It is a grand and significant occasion: the divine Father, having called in all orders of his subject angels from the immensity of his kingdom, announces the exaltation of his radiant Son to the position and power of deputy Creator and Ruler of all created universes. This proclamation is greeted by august hymns of praise from reverential angels, who bow with veiled faces in worship and dance intricate measures joyously. God rejoices at their joy. (It is reported that Urania, together with her sister Wisdom, has also played in the presence of the Almighty Father, pleased with her celestial song.) I have watched in bewilderment and some embarrassment the Giant-Angels as they dispose themselves, after daylong dancing, on beds of flowers around a table piled with Angels' food, eating in full measure but not to excess and in sweet communion drinking the fruit of Heaven's vines. Later sociable Raphael explains to Adam how these intelligential substances can taste, concoct, digest, and assimilate even the coarser victuals fit for human consumption and, blushing a celestial rosy red, reveals how Spirits embrace in lovemaking without obstacle of membrane, joint or limb. It is a pure Love somewhat like Adam's. And it is suggested to Adam that, with right living in strict obedience to God, his body may at last turn all to spirit or become ethereal such as the bodily substance of angels. But not all angels in Heaven are reverential. Lucifer the Archangel, called Satan, conspires against the Almighty. And drawing after him one-third of the angelic hosts, he marches over illimitable distances into the North, where he prepares to establish himself in his pride as a King equal to his Divine Master. I, too, have many times followed him and his hosts into the regions of the North.

Three days of battle centering around Satan's stronghold are impressive. Here one may hear the arms of Giant-Angels clashing horrible discord on rock-of-diamond armor, the raging of brazen chariots, and the hiss of fiery arrows: Uriel, Abdiel, and Raphael fight individual foes with distinction, and Michael with tempered sword shears away Satan's right side in a wound which heals instantly after bleeding nectarous humor; and at the end of the first-day battle all the ground is strewn with shivered armor and heaps of chariots, charioteers, and fiery steeds. The second day of battle is characterized by two astonishing marvels. On the night previous Satan and his crew might be observed mining an enormous crater in the very floor of Heaven, down through several strata—one of mineral and stone—to the originals of Nature in their crude conception—that is to chaos itself—where they discover desired materials of sulphurous and fiery nature. From these, powder is concocted and adusted; from minerals, cannons and chained thunderbolts of iron globes are manufactured. In the morning fearful cannonading fells the Almighty's angels by thousands upon the fields of battle, amazed and near defeat. But recovering they find available mountains, hills, and promontories which, being torn from their foundations, are hurled upon the rebel hosts. Feeling the near disastrous effects of such ammunition, Satan's forces also pluck up and cast other hills, and Heaven rings with the infernal noise of hill exploding against hill in midair. There are as yet no victors; angels, being of equal ethereal nature, cannot destroy each other. On the third morning, however, the Almighty Father's own Son is dispatched to conquer the accursed rebels. He is provided with the Paternal Deity's marvelous chariot, flashing thick flames, wheel within wheel, itself instinct with spirit, undrawn but convoyed by four cherubic Shapes; he is accompanied by ten thousand Saints and armed with three-bolted thunder. First, at his command the uprooted hills retire to their usual places, the devastated landscape is repaired, and Heaven's wonted face is renewed. As he approaches the enemy, the Empyrean shakes throughout, except the throne of God, under the burning wheels of his chariot. And the enemy, terrified by his angry countenance and the lightning of his power, throw down their arms, and in utter defeat suffer the chariot wheels to roll over them. They are rooted out of Heaven, cast into the middle darkness of chaos, and pursued by warrior-angels to the mouth of a prepared Hell. The Son returns triumphant to the Father in mid-Heaven.

These peccant angels have often been my companions in the fall through the tenfold confusion and terrifying noises of the Hoary Deep. It is a dark illimitable ocean of conflicting forces, where the mysterious presence of Chaos and Old Night, ancestors of Nature, rule and hold eternal anarchy. Here the pregnant causes of all created universes are mixed confusedly, awaiting the Mighty Maker's hand. I have many times wondered about its origin and have sought, without success, some golden reed with which to measure its hyperbolical infinitude. With unflagging fascination and admiration I have traced Satan's upward flight through warring atoms to the precincts of Light. I have watched with unfailing astonishment the monsters, Sin and Death, as they build an allegorical highway through and over the unimaginable expanses of chaos-space. Here is ancientry supreme, but movements of inexhaustible energies released here prophesy unlimited combinations of matter and form in all future creations.

Hell is no pleasant place. But its present inhabitants for whom it was perhaps recently established provide the attentive observer with elements of consolation. Here may be discovered whirlwinds of tempestuous flames—"yet from those flames / No light, but rather darkness visible"—landscapes and lakes burning with solid or liquid fire, multiplied and terrifying agencies of misery-producing torture without end. Such scenes are entirely worthy of the inspired artist's imagination and representation. But the manner in which Satan and his followers suffer defeat, undergo horrid punishment, and face ultimate tragedy is also worthy of unmixed admiration. They are mightily fallen, to be sure, but Oh how changed! One tends to feel little concern for their loss of former brightness of body, though Satan weeps bitter tears of remorse and compassion when he beholds how the glory of his faithful companions is withered. But there are compensations: they can rejoice at having escaped what they consider the tyranny of Heaven and the subservience required of them there; they have achieved a freedom which, in democratic fashion, permits expression of independent, personal opinion on vital questions; unlike human beings, they can at last rest and act in unanimous accord; their unlimited energies are cheerfully and freely employed in rearing a magnificent structure of gold to the sound of dulcet symphonies and sweet voices; like their leader, they have been inspired with the glory of a courage which supports an unconquerable will never to submit or yield. With democratic initiative they would now set about making in some sense a Heaven of Hell. Such is the fashion in which men and angels alike should endure the blows of tragic experience. It is extremely regrettable, however, that these excellences of mind and spirit should be vitiated and corrupted by an unclean desire for revenge.

Meantime, while Satan pursues his successful voyage from Hell through chaos to Earth, these intelligential creatures and I often entertain many hours together in recreational companionship or in expeditions of discovery and high adventure. Some engage in athletic contests, in feats of mock battle, or in races with chariots drawn by fiery steeds rivaling the Olympian games. Some retreat to a silent valley where they sing with angelic notes to many a harp—like the ancient scops—their own heroic deeds or lament the hapless fall of heroes doomed by Fate; such harmony, though partial, suspends Hell and ravishes the audience. Others in more elevated vein reason about Providence, Will and free choice, Fate, the effects of foreknowledge—and, like human beings lost in similar mazes, find no solutions; but the pleasing sorcery of philosophical contemplation charms pain for awhile and arms the hardened heart with patience. Others with more élan set out on expeditions to discover what mysteries lie within the regions of bottomless Hell. Our adventure is amply rewarded: we sight four infernal rivers— Styx, Acheron, Cocytus, fierce Phlegeton, and far beyond these, Lethe, the river of oblivion. Beyond their flood stretches a frozen continent beat with perpetual storms of hail which, never thawing, gathers with snow and ice into an ancient pile so frore that cold performs the effect of fire, even of black fire. In these dolorous regions all life dies, death lives, and perverse Nature breeds the monsters and abominable prodigies later known to human legend and myth. My companions, however, survive the hardships of these explorations. They return with undiminished ardor to greet with others the arrival in Pandemonium of their Mighty Chief, hear with exuberant laughter how he has successfully seduced Man to destruction, and to suffer with him a serpentine debasement of form. Through long association with these denizens of Hell I have grown to respect their verve, bounce, and resilience of mind; they seem to have been rejuvenated in this place and, in their proper forms, to glow with the forward-looking spirit of eternal youth. But one shudders with horror to imagine what will happen when they escape to the mountains, plains, and purlieus of Earth.

II

Travel through the four main entities of the limitless space of Milton's *Paradise Lost*—created Heaven, Hell, the World, and emanated chaos—may be highly entertaining or instructive, but it can never completely satisfy the questing mind. At every turn innumerable questions throng to the bar of penetrant thought demanding just answers: Precisely how, for what purpose, out of what materials, and according to what structural pattern was the World created? What imagination was powerful enough to conceive its foundations and release energies sufficient to control the mechanics of its complex motions? Who or what sustains its continued existence? Is the ethereal Heaven of Heavens of material origin? If so, why should an omnipresent Deity set up his throne in this particular place? Are the bodies of angels composed of form and sublimated matter without being subject to dissolution? Can Man's body attain such perfection? From what Spirit emanated the substrate of prime matter in chaos? Who prepared its chaotic elements for creation of all universes? Was it indeed the gentle mind of the Almighty's Son which designed and fabricated out of prepared materials the continents of horror in the expanse of Hell? Is it possible to describe or define the metaphysical essences of God, Son, and Holy Spirit as they function in processes of creation? Or to make definitive the entities of all visible and invisible substances? Such are a few of the questions which continually besiege the mind of the traveler. And answers do not always prove to be available because inquiries into the nature of ultimate realities must necessarily be partial in effect or indeed sometimes abortive.

Inquisitive scholars and critics, bent upon investigation and interpretation of only these four sections of *Paradise Lost*, are likely at first to be overwhelmed by the avalanche of Milton's released knowledge and to be astonished by his apparent haphazard use of it. Here Christian traditions of all sorts are jumbled with classical mythology and philosophy, with rabbinical interpretation of sacred books, with atomistic, orphic, and scholastic speculation, and with Neoplatonic theology in what seems to be a wild disorder. Here St. Augustine, St. Basil, and St. Thomas rub shoulders, if only at some distance, with Epicurus, Lucretius, and Democritus; Hesiod furnishes mysterious names of gods, foreign to Ezekiel and John of Patmos; Damascius, Epimenides, and Proclus provide symbolic figures unknown to Plato or Aristotle or Hermes Trismegistus; Greek Tartarus and Christian Inferno are reflected in Hell; pagan gods from many legends are metamorphosed into the demons of Christian tradition. Any industrious source-hunter may well become bewildered by such a hodgepodge of fragments, echoes, reflected jots and tittles from this or that originally unrelated system of philosophy, and by the plethora of allusions to myths and legends never so associated before. Dr. Johnson's sense of being overburdened is understandable. I myself have often come to this conclusion: Milton is an eclectic without any great ability to systematize his fascinating materials.

Fortunately for me, however, my education in Milton's methodologies employed in *Paradise Lost* has been progressive. Upon more mature consideration it appears to me now that he is an original thinker in his own right and that he incorporates in his well-conceived epic plans a foison of imaginative and philosophical treasures, gleaned from a tremendous variety of incompatible sources but carefully ordered to serve his specific purposes. He will not subject himself completely to any previous or contemporary system of thought, though he may use such elements, pro and con, as seem desirable. For example, at times he seems to be a Platonist, but he will not adopt Plato's idealistic system as a whole. He may approve some Aristotelian concepts, but on another occasion he may find it advisable to condemn Aristotle. On the origin of matter he can be said, in general, to favor emanation, though he will not unreservedly follow the fantastic imaginings of Plotinus or even of Proclus to whom he is closest related. In representing creation of the World he is undoubtedly a confirmed atomist, but his concepts are not precisely like those of Democritus or Epicurus or of Comenius and other contemporaries. In structure the Mundane Universe is geocentric, but the familiar *Primum Mobile* of the Ptolemaic cosmology is replaced by a stationary shell. Now it is one function of the sincere scholar, we may agree, to garner diligently all available facts involved in the source materials which Milton employs, to render clear the original positions of such facts in their respective systems or traditions, and to observe what changes or alterations have been made in the process of fitting them for new relationships. For one may be sure that whatever Milton touches straightway becomes Miltonic. Even floods of conflicting influences —to be carefully distinguished from direct sources—receive the transforming magic of his original thought and are reconciled by the power of his discursive reason. I must conclude at this stage, therefore, that Milton is a most distinguished and successful syncretist.

Still it has seemed to me at times that the three well-ordered entities under consideration are perhaps unnecessarily crammed with furniture and adornment, however

splendid. Within a comparatively flimsy containing shell of
the World, for example, are packed our Earth with abundant
flora and fauna, the spheres of all the planets and fixed stars,
lower waters, and beyond all these the protective "upper
waters" of the Crystalline ocean. Heaven of Heavens has
its mountains, plains, and rivers, its towers, its tremendous
armies and battles of armed angels, its Hill of infinite Deity
himself cramped within the confines of a circumscribed wall.
Hell would seem to be overcrowded—though said to be
bottomless—with lakes of fire and burning shores, with its
mountains of metallic ores, its dark rivers flowing from unknown sources into fiery seas, with its broad continents of
eternal cold, and its inhabitants consisting in number of a
third of all created intelligential substances. Perhaps no-
body might be disposed to question the superb quality and
arrangement of these magnificent furnishings. It is only
that the containing room or space seems too small to com-
pass them without giving the impression of congestion.
Consequently, Milton's epic style seems at times to be forced
as if perhaps under some pressure to satisfy the demands
of a more nearly infinite space. As usual, however, the apparent fault in this situation has proved to be not Milton's
but mine. The fact is simply that my comparatively restricted mind does not function adequately within the limitless spaciousness of Milton's mind; my imagination is not
sufficiently alive and expanded to conceive, except dimly,
the hyperbolical infinitudes of space with which his imagination has invested the contents of these three created universes. But I have made some progress in understanding.
Under Miltonic stimulation my mental vision registers a
somewhat expanded, though still expanding, spacial horizon;
my quickened imagination reports that elements of the

room-contents, while maintaining their original happy relationships, have gradually receded from each other to the point where there is no longer any indication of congestion. No limit to the poet's imaginative concepts is discoverable, but I am sure they are so vast that even to suggest their significance he must resort to symbols of appropriate magnitudes.

Symbols of any proportions must necessarily be baffling to the interpreter. As Bunyan says cryptically, "metaphors make us blind." Sometimes the very nature of the symbol is so uncertain or unstable or abstract that it resists analysis and definition. It is therefore subject to an unlimited variety of interpretations of its inner meaning or what it represents. Psychologically speaking, a "true" interpretation is scarcely possible: a symbol comes freshly chosen from the poet's mind with a penumbra of his strictly personal associations about it and with memories of his individual experiences thick upon it; the interpreter achieves no true interpretation partly because he can never understand the complexities which urged the original choice but mainly because the complexion of the symbol is bound to be conditioned in his mind by its assimilation to his own associations and experiences. Or sometimes a total representation may be of such unimaginable proportions that one hesitates to class it as symbolic at all. For example, I am continually pursued by the suspicion that the material but invisible Heaven of Heavens may possibly be considered a symbol of ineffable spiritual realities concealed in the Light which surrounds the throne of Deity and that Hell, including the allegorical figures, Sin and Death, may represent symbolically the origin, unclean nature, and horrible effects of Evil. Such speculations may admittedly be only vagaries. But there are two of Milton's grandest symbols which for me are particularly perplexing and difficult.

First, in the midst of the indescribable turmoil and darkness of chaos Satan discovers two mysterious divinities, Chaos and Sable-vested Night. These spirits of the nethermost Abyss sit enthroned, spreading wide their dark pavilion, ruling and subsisting by virtue of the anarchy about them. They are masculine and feminine aspects of the same reality. But as usual in cosmogonies, the symbol itself defies full analysis because it seems unstable, fluctuating in this case between some sort of metaphysical principles and human personality. On the other hand, any cosmogonal existence in process of becoming is so limitless in extent and so recondite that no symbol, however occult or unstable, is capable of representing it adequately. Still, Chaos and Old Night may in general be glimpsed as symbolizing, if not too clearly, various stages in the mystic emanation of materiality from pure spirituality. Specifically, they represent the last emanation, prime matter, and the inexhaustible potentialities, qualities, motions in space of that obscure composite body, chaos. I say "obscure" composite body because chaos with its substrate of matter can be considered as next to the last emanation or as an evolution of prime matter divinely prepared for the reception of forms in all processes of creation. In either case, this complex existence as symbolized by Chaos and Old Night is the womb of that Nature which assumes sovereignty over the Mundane Universe— and may perhaps become her grave. In all my travels through Milton's universes I have not been able to escape completely from the toils of chaos and its substrate, matter. Heaven of Heavens seems in its ethereal splendor farthest removed, but Satan discloses as he mines its floor that it rests on chaotic materials out of which its beauties have been sublimated. Every physical property of Hell bears upon it the signature of chaos. In the company of Raphael I have seen the Filial Godhead descend into turbulent chaos and with his golden compasses circumscribe the limits of the Cosmos to be. And this same Raphael, in his hylomorphic Scale of Nature, seems to postulate that from one first matter have been evolved all phenomena of creation: various degrees of substance and in things that live of life, in Man not only vital spirits but also fancy, understanding, and the human soul, which as final sublimation of matter receives discursive reason. Even the intelligential substance of angels—they possess and exercise intuitive reason—is of precisely the same kind as Man's, differing only in a more spiritous degree of purity. Thus in some instances the universal body works up to spirit. Faced with such considerations and with the statement elsewhere that all things are produced by or from "the power of matter," I have often been distressed to conclude that Milton is a crass materialist and that, whatever his religious views may be, his spiritual insight seems to need enlightenment.

But such myopic complaint has just as often been medicined by contemplation upon the most ineffable of all symbols, Light and its component Darkness. In a consideration of the Light-symbol, multiplying complexities and mysteries swarm upon the interpreter. For example, God is defined as being essentially a Spirit; rooted in his essence may be discerned his attributes, among which are oneness, immutability, and omnipresence. And because such properties cannot be compassed by the human mind, Milton like many others must employ the mystic concept, God is Light and has dwelt in unapproached Light from eternity. This abstract Spirit is therefore omnipresent as Light. But since both Spirit and symbolical Light are incomprehensible, God as metaphysical Entity must remain the impenetrable Monad. The Almighty Father in his creative capacity, however, is omniscient, omnipotent, gracious and merciful, just in his judgments, abounding in vitality, wisdom, and truth; God is Love. Pouring forth his creative energies through successive stages and agencies, this Eternal King is the source from whom all things proceed. He is the Fountain of all Light which is the effluence—perhaps in the form of a pure Ethereal Stream or a coeternal Beam—of his bright uncreated essence. These mysteries are perplexing to Milton himself, but it is clear that Light can be said to symbolize not only the Being of that omnipresent Spirit who is sometimes named Jehovah but also all manifestations of emanating powers or energies of God conceived as Eternal King. It is therefore fitting that in Heaven of Heavens the Almighty Father should be represented as sitting, himself invisible, upon an inaccessible throne surrounded by a cloud of glorious brightness blazing like a radiant shrine. His excessively bright skirts symbolize of course the mantling of his divine glories and energies. It is also appropriate that his only Son—recently named Creator and Ruler of all created universes—should appear as the radiant image and effulgence of the Father's glory, in whose shining countenance is made visible the invisible deity of the Almighty Father. The Son so endowed has created Heaven of Heavens flooded with a creative Light which produces and sustains its ethereal grandeurs; its angelic inhabitants are with reason called Spirits of Purest Light or Progeny of Light or Sons of Light. After the Son has delimited the chaotic gobe which is to become the World, there is a mysterious Darkness upon the face of the Deep. But when he says, "Let there be Light," instantly Light exhaling first from Darkness appears visibly in the East and as creative energy circles the mass on three successive days; on the fourth day this Light is gathered into the Sun's body, whence it continues to rule and sustain the radiant Mundane Universe. There is no indication available as to how Hell was suddenly at need produced. But since the Filial Godhead is the Creator of all things, he must have created it with all its dark horrors including its flames from which comes no light but rather visible Darkness. The essential relationship between Light and Darkness is exceedingly recondite. Ordinarily darkness may be considered merely absence of light. But in *Paradise Lost* they seem often to be created essences or components of one essence. (In Isaiah the Lord says, "I form the light, and create darkness.") These two entities are so merged that there does not appear to exist any visible or invisible Light without some touch of Darkness or any Darkness without some trace of Light.* As the *Zohar* has it explicitly: "Both are one in kind, as there is no light without darkness and no darkness without light; but though one, they are different in color." Even in Heaven of Heavens, for example, the excessive brightness of God's skirts seems dark, and Mammon remembers that sometimes Heaven's King covers his throne with dark clouds and with the "majesty of darkness" so that Heaven resembles Hell. The so-called "utter Darkness" of Hell itself is illumined by the blaze of Cherubim's flaming swords, the conference "temple" is lighted as from a sky by starry lamps and blazing cressets, and the burning soil is not without the hidden lustre of gems and gold. The form of

---

* In the Appendix I have pursued this enigma to what some may consider fantastic extremes.

Hell's dread Commander, though shorn of much original brightness, still shines in somewhat obscured glory. But Light and Darkness are separable: in Heaven there is a cave under God's mount where Light and Darkness lodge and dislodge by turns; on the first day of creation, we have seen visible Light exhaling from its component Darkness; and finally on this same day God divides light from darkness. But aside from some of the foregoing speculative paradoxes, Light is in many circumstances the traditional and universal symbol representing spiritual goodness, truth, or divine beauty; its contrary, Darkness, symbolizes spiritual depravity and all manifestations of evil.

That incorporeal Spirit who is Light and the Source of all Light has hounded me throughout the unbounded expanse of Miltonic space. There is no escape; he is omniscient and omnipresent. The Almighty himself says, "I am who fill Infinitude," adding the corollary, "nor vacuous the space." In Heaven of Heavens he is, as we have seen, the All-ruling Sire clothed in eternal Light. If Beelzebub and the Psalmist make their beds in Hell, behold he is there; for be sure that, in height or depth, still first and last he reigns sole King. Chaos manifests his emanated substance and power. In the created Cosmos I have watched with awe how his divine breath or Light, as transmitted by the Son and other servants, dispenses an omnipresent life and sustaining energy which penetrates and runs through all created essences. His omniscience compasses all that has been or can be. In addition, I have felt a more mystic and disturbing Presence, an all-pervading Spirit who is everywhere in total space at the same time—"for where is He not present"? When the Son, after creation of the World, returns to sit by the Father, it is said of the latter, "He also went invisible, yet stayed—such is the privilege of Omnipresence." Though the concepts of omniscience and omnipresence may be incomprehensible, they do suggest that the combined essences, forces, motions, laws, elements, and qualities of Heaven, Hell, chaos, and the Cosmos—everything contained in total space—can in sum be conceived as constituting the Being of God. Such fearful considerations have led me to conclude reluctantly that Milton may be a spiritual pantheist.

Such a desperate conclusion regarding pantheism in *Paradise Lost*, however, is not necessarily valid. Milton does indeed situate each of his created universes and chaos in its own individual and almost infinite space-continuum or plenum. All these entities exist in an unbroken relationship to each other by virtue of that one first matter which is common to all. And that Divine Spirit who is Light does fill as a mystic presence each of these nonvacuous spaces. But for two reasons this is not Miltonic pantheism. In the first place, a pantheistic concept of nature is frequently dependent upon a limited point of view and a restricted experience. For example, an earthbound man may look upon a sunset or the ocean or the blue sky and experience a mystic sense that here is present an indwelling Something deeply interfused; he may conclude that this moving Spirit runs through and controls all things. He can interpret his experience, therefore, as meaning that this Spirit is Nature or that all manifestations of nature constitute God. But Milton is not such a man; his eye glances from Heaven to Hell, from chaos to Earth, and his experience is vastly more profound. He is aware, in the second place, of what I have called total space which compasses the individual spaces of Heaven, Hell, chaos, and the World. The characteristics of this Miltonic total space are similar to those attributed to our actual three-

dimensional space by modern scientists. Sir Arthur Edding-
ton in *The Expanding Universe,* for example, explains that
all space is curved, closed but unbounded, and that the
whole volume of spherical space is finite. Beyond this there
is—nothing! So it is with Milton's sphere of total space; it
too is curved, closed but boundless, and finite. He differs
from modern scientists, however, in assuming that "beyond"
and "around" the sphere of total space there subsists that
Deity who is Light; for God says, it will be remembered,
"I am who fill Infinitude." Thus all things closed in finite
total space are "within" the infinitude of Deity, who must
therefore be omnipresent in that space as well as being infinitely omnipresent.* His presence in all space is not pantheism; for want of a better term, I will venture to call it
theopantism.

Regarding the essential qualities of John Milton, I must
conclude that he is one of the most spiritual of men. He
has entered into the adytum of the ultimate Mysteries where
we ordinary mortals may well hesitate to follow. With un-
daunted heart he faces Infinitude and the near-infinite.
Though in controversy with men he is independent revealing a pride that seems to approach arrogance, yet as searcher
after eternal truth he is humble. With deep reverence he
appeals for instruction and illumination of mind to that
Spirit which prefers above all temples the pure and upright
heart. As if with bowed head he beseeches Celestial Light
to shine inward and, as he says

>   the mind through all her powers
> Irradiate, there plant eyes, all mist from thence
> Purge and disperse, that I may see and tell
> Of things invisible to mortal sight.

* For a crude representation of this situation, see the graph on page 156.

The limitless sweep of his creative imagination compasses all space, and his unmisted inward eyes behold and render clear its complex contents. Thus he has created the grandest of all stages upon which to present the most spiritually profound of all plays known to man.* In structure the stage itself is unique—nothing is discoverable in earlier or later times precisely comparable—its floors being of sufficient magnitude and strength to support the tread of titanic actors. And both stage and play are brightly illuminated by that Light which fills Infinitude. But it must be confessed again that my associations with this Milton are not always comfortable; the dignity of his spirit and the sternness of his purposes do not facilitate easy companionship, though he is human. Still he is—in the apt words of an American poet—"A soul admitted to itself" and as such must remain in essence "Impregnable of inquest however neighborly."

* The playbill is impressive: it announces a great argument involving the purpose to assert Eternal Providence and justify the ways of God to men. Here may be seen the creation of Man, his temptation and fall into sin, his redemption thence, and his possible entrance into glory at the Second Coming of the Redeemer. Final dissolution of the World is emphasized, and the swallowing up of Time in Eternity is envisioned.

Chapter 1

THE PURPOSE OF THIS CHAPTER IS TO DISENGAGE MIL-
ton's philosophy of the divine nature from narrow
theological or sectarian controversy and to show how consistently his dual concept of the Deity in relation to the
world is developed in the *Christian Doctrine* and embodied
in *Paradise Lost.*

In the *Christian Doctrine*[1] Milton approaches his consideration of God with due reverence and humility, confessing
readily that it is "impossible to comprehend accurately under
any form of definition the 'divine nature'" (XIV, 39). Still,
"the Deity has imprinted upon the human mind so many
unquestionable tokens of himself, and so many traces of him
are apparent throughout the whole of nature," that one may
arrive at some imperfect concept of him by intuition and
the exercise of reason (XIV, 25). Milton does not himself
intuit God in the mystic union of the human intelligence
with the superintellectual principle, as Plotinus and others
do.[2] But he does depend largely upon reports of those who,

MILTON'S DUAL CONCEPT OF GOD AS RELATED TO CREATION

in the Sacred Scriptures, have had visions and revelations granted them by Christ in various ages concerning the nature of Deity. And these disclosures the philosopher interprets with no inconsiderable originality by the exercise of reason in the application of metaphysical principles. He finds by diligent searching of the Scriptures that God's nature may be partially apprehended by reference to descriptions of his revealed attributes. And in arranging the order of these properties he is cognizant of the fact that the Deity may be considered in two ways: namely, (1) in the mode of his metaphysical subsistence, and (2) in the mode of his operational existence, or as the Efficient Cause of all concrete effects.

I

From the metaphysical point of view God is said to be an "*ens* in the abstract" (XIV, 43) or the "primary ens of all"

(XIV, 221). That is to say, he is a Being (ontos), *that which is, that which is in itself and through itself,* and as such it is one of the transcendentals and cannot be defined. Milton notes three names which seem to intimate this most recondite nature of Deity: Jehovah, " 'he who is,' or 'which is, and which was, and which is to come' "; Jah, a sort of contraction of Jehovah having the same significance; and Ehie, " 'I am that I am,' or 'will be' " (XIV, 39, 41). Now in order to comprehend the attributes of this Being, it is necessary to consider his essence, or the essence of the abstract Ens. Essence has been defined as "something primary in the thing and the root of all its properties; that which is conceived first in the thing without which the thing cannot be . . . ; the essence is conceived in the concept of the thing and stated in its *definition.*"[3] Or as St. Thomas Aquinas has it, "Essence is what is expressed by the definition."[4] Since God's essence is, according to definition, the root of all his properties, Milton proceeds to define God, considered in his essential nature, as a Spirit. He continues:

Whence it is evident that the essence of God, being in itself most simple, can admit no compound quality; so that the term *hypostasis* Heb. i. 3. which is differently translated *substance,* or *subsistence,* or *person,* can be nothing else but that most perfect essence by which God subsists by himself, in himself, and through himself. For neither *substance* nor *subsistence* makes any addition to what is already a most perfect essence; and the word *person* in its later acceptation signifies any individual thing gifted with intelligence, whereas *hypostasis* denotes not the *ens* itself, but the essence of the *ens* in the abstract. *Hypostasis,* therefore, is clearly the same as essence, and thus many of the Latin commentators render it in the passage already quoted. Therefore, as God is a most simple essence, so is he also a most simple subsistence (XIV, 41, 43).

Having established that the most simple essence of God is identical with his *substance* or *subsistence* or *hypostasis,* the controversalist finds that "there can be no real difference of meaning between the adverbs *essentially* and *substantially*" (XIV, 221). If these terms be applied to God alone, they must also be applied to God the Father alone, "since one substantial essence means nothing else than one hypostasis, and vice versa" (XIV, 221). He continues:

I would therefore ask my adversaries, whether they hold the Father to be an abstract ens or not? Questionless they will reply, the primary ens of all. I answer, therefore, that as he is one hypostasis, so must he have one essence proper to himself, incommunicable in the highest degree, and participated by no one, that is, by no person besides, for he cannot have his own proper hypostasis, without having his own proper essence. For it is impossible for any ens to retain its own essence in common with any other thing whatever, since by this essence it is what it is, and is numerically distinguished from all others (XIV, 221).

This conclusion is further supported by reference to another property rooted in God's simple essence: namely, his unity. All evidence from the Sacred Scriptures indicates that there subsists "numerically one God and one Spirit, in the common acceptation of numerical unity" (XIV, 51). Aristotle had pointed out that " 'to be one' means 'to be indivisible' (being essentially a particular thing, distinct and separate in place or form or thought), or 'to be whole and indivisible.' "[5] St. Thomas agrees that "the reason why any singular thing is *this particular thing* is because it cannot be communicated to many" and argues that because of God's simplicity he is one.[6] And Ralph Cudworth declares: "From the idea of God . . . it evidently appears that there can be but one such thing, and that . . . unity, oneliness, or singularity is essential to it."[7] And Milton emphasizes that "nothing can be said of the one God, which is inconsistent with his unity, and which assigns to him at the same time attributes of unity and plurality" (XIV, 51).

Other attributes of the Deity are truth, immensity, infinity, and as a consequence of his infinity, his omnipresence (XIV, 41, 43, 47). His eternity implies that he has neither beginning nor end; and related to his eternity are his immutability and incorruptibility (XIV, 43, 47). Such are the attributes which describe the nature of God in the mode of his metaphysical subsistence. And considered in this manner he is indeed incomprehensible.

For here is represented an extremely recondite Abstraction, an Ens so mysterious that it is beyond definition; one can only say that it exists in itself and through itself. Its essence is defined in such abstract terms that the human mind can scarcely comprehend their full significance. Here is God, the ineffable Spirit, eternal, infinite, immutable, and incorruptible locked securely, as it were, within an impenetrable numerical unity. He has some recognizable affinity with Aristotle's First Principle, which is impartible, impassive, unalterable, eternal, and immovable.[8] Milton's God is above or beyond the category of relation (except perhaps in respect to his omnipresence), wrapped within himself in a sort of "frozen passivity" or eternal rest, resembling in some sense the Absolute of the Neoplatonists.[9] No man has seen God; even to Moses was revealed only the Eternal's "hinder parts." The flagging thought of man must fall back upon the sublime symbol, "God is Light." So Milton is at great pains to defend the inviolability and the incommunicability of God's essence. And thus he seems to precipitate himself into a philosophical dilemma and Deity into a metaphysical plight. For God is said to have generated a Son, and it is an article of faith that he created, among other things, a visible universe. How can this be?

II

Now when we come to consider God in his divine power and excellence as the Efficient Cause of all possible effects, an entirely different group of attributes must be formulated. For here are involved multifarious and complicated relationships of both an internal and an external nature. Here God's vitality is emphasized; he is the "living God" who is therefore the source of all life (XIV, 55). He is not merely an abstract Person or substance; he is or has intelligence, by means of which he knows all thoughts of the children of men and searches all hearts. His omniscience is universal (XIV, 55). And, perhaps most important of all, as regards the will of God, he is infinitely pure and holy, most gracious, merciful and long-suffering, abounding in goodness and truth, infinitely wise, faithful, and just in his judgments (XIV, 57, 59). God is love. "From all these attributes springs that infinite excellence which constitutes the true perfection of God, and causes him to abound in glory, and to be most deservedly and justly the supreme Lord of all things" (XIV, 61). Thus God is a Monarch who, provided with vitality, intelligence, and will, produces and rules all things. He must, therefore, be styled by us wonderful.

Though the essence of God is impartible and immovable, nevertheless as Efficient Cause he exercises intelligence and will in the employment of infinite power to produce multifarious effects. His decrees, internal and external, are entirely independent of external agency. Whatever he has decreed from all eternity of his own most free and wise purpose, precludes the possibility of his being in any sense controlled by necessity (XIV, 63, 65). Among his special decrees, we are here concerned primarily with that which has to do with his generation of a Son, whence is derived his name of Father. And the generation of the Son, representing the execution of a decree, must be considered as an example of his external efficiency, since the Father and Son are different persons, each possessing his own individual essence (XIV, 179, 181). Then just precisely how does God produce the Son?

This question, Milton confesses, is naturally a great mystery and very obscure. His theological adversaries argue that there is a certain emanation, or procession, spiration, or issuing of the Son from the Father (XIV, 181), but he himself is not too certain of the problem's solution. Indeed, he finds very few texts in Sacred Scriptures relating to the Son's generation or production. At any rate, he will have nothing to do with the celebrated "homoousian," or the concept of three hypostases rooted in a single essence;[10] distinctions involved in the orthodox conception of the Trinity are mere verbal quibbles, "founded on the use of synonymous words, and cunningly dressed up in terms borrowed from the Greek to dazzle the eyes of novices" (XIV, 221). He will rather hold strenuously to his own views: namely, the essence of the Father cannot be communicated to another person; the Son is distinguished also in his own essence; and "since a numerical difference originates in difference of essence, those who are two numerically, must be also two essentially" (XIV, 203). The Son, therefore, cannot possibly be coessential with God the Father: he is clearly a subordinate and independent essence produced as an effect by the will of God, from whom all things proceed. Moreover, the Son is not coeternal with the Father. No physical necessity impelled the generation of the Son; but since he is the consequence of a freewill decree, he was begotten within the limits of time (XIV, 187). Without employing too much metaphysical "trifling," one must recognize that he was originally in the bosom of the Father and proceeded from him (XIV, 253), which implies a certain potentiality in God; and "if he was originally in the Father, but now exists separately, he has undergone a certain change at some time or other, and is therefore mutable" (XIV, 309).

Milton now proceeds to inquire how or in what sense God the Father can have begotten such a Son. He finds that this point can be "easily explained" by reference to the Scriptures; for when the Only Begotten is called *"the first born of every creature,* and *the beginning of the creation of God,"* it is clearly evident that "God of his own will created, or generated, or produced the Son before all things, endued with the divine nature." He continues:

The generation of the divine nature is described by no one with more sublimity and copiousness than by the apostle in Hebrews, i. 2, 3. "whom he hath appointed heir of all things, by whom also he made the worlds; who being the brightness of his glory, and the express image of his person," &c. It must be understood from this, that God imparted to the Son as much as he pleased of the divine nature, nay of the divine substance itself, care being taken not to confound the substance with the whole essence, which would imply, that the Father had given to the Son what he retained numerically the same himself; which would be a contradiction of terms instead of a mode of generation. This is the whole that is revealed concerning the generation of the Son of God (XIV, 193).

This passage needs to be scanned carefully and in some detail. Milton's whole theory appears in danger of disintegration. In the production of the Son's metaphysical entity or essence or quiddity, the Father is said to have imparted to the "express image of his person" as much of his "divine substance" as pleased him, though not his "whole essence." The enthusiastic controversialist has already explained that in reference to God the terms *substance* and *essence* (hence *substantiality* and *essentiality*) have precisely the same meaning and that God's essence (and so his substance) is indivisible and incommunicable to any other person. But it here appears that God does communicate as much of his substance as pleases him; and the term *whole* (tota) would seem to imply that he imparts at least some of his essence, at the same time retaining his numerical unity himself. The solution of this paradox is not easily discoverable. But Milton is no doubt familiar with Aristotle and the Scholastic philosophers and is fully aware that the term *substance* may have at least two different meanings. As Aristotle says, "Thus it follows that 'substance' has two senses: the ultimate subject, which cannot be further predicated of something else; and whatever has an individual and separate existence."[11] And St. Thomas develops this idea in detail: "In one sense it [substance] means the quiddity of a thing, signified by its definition, and thus we say that the definition means the substance of a thing; in which sense substance is called by the Greeks *ousia*, which we may call *essence*." Milton understands substance in this sense when he says that God's *substance* and *essence* mean the same thing. St. Thomas continues in the same passage: "In another sense substance means a subject or *suppositum*, which subsists in a genus of substance. To this, taken in a general sense, can be applied a name expressive of an intention; and thus it is called the *suppositum*."[12] In other words, as I understand it, when we come to consider how the multifarious essences of individual things flow as effects from the First and Efficient Cause, the cognoscitive faculty must establish by supposition or premise an underlying principle or "substance" which is subject to change. As McKeon says, "It is the property of substance that, remaining the same in number itself, it may undergo contraries; it is not itself susceptible of a contrary, nor of more or less, although it is the subject of both in change or mutation."[13] Just as, according to the principle of the so-called "solidarity" of the human race, the whole of human nature is present in each individual man,[14] so we must suppose that the divine nature of God (substance in the second sense) is imparted to the Son. Milton no doubt has this sense of substance in mind when he speaks of Christ's having "received his fulness from God" or all the "fulness of the Godhead bodily"; for, says he, "the term 'bodily,' which is subjoined . . . means 'substantially'" (XIV, 339). Thus the Father has generated in the Son an express image of his person—even as man is created in his image (XIV, 275)—and has imparted to him as much as he pleased of his substance (in the second sense, implying mutation and change) while retaining his substance (in the first sense, essence, *ousia*) in numerical unity. Such is the divine nature of the Son as a metaphysical entity.

The essence of the Son—being the independent effect of generation—may be likened to a mirror, as it were, which reflects faithfully the "form of God" (XIV, 343); he is the "image" of the Father's person. The Son, therefore, has imparted to him many reflected attributes which describe the divine nature of God—but not all of them. In fact, being definitely a subordinate person and merely an image, the Son participates scarcely at all in the Father's metaphysical attributes: he is mutable, finite, and in a sense corruptible—only God is immutable, infinite, and incorruptible; he is not absolutely omnipresent (XIV, 317), because omnipresence is a consequence of infinity; having been generated in "time," he cannot be eternal—only God has neither beginning nor end; and he cannot infringe upon the inviolable unity of God. But just as the Father exists also as Final and Efficient Cause of all operations, so the Son functions as secondary cause in creation and as mediator between God and man. For the exercise of these functions, the Son must be generously invested with attributes of his own similar to those which reveal the Father's power and excellence. Though omniscience belongs to the Father alone—"the Son . . . knows not all things absolutely" (XIV, 317)—together with supreme domain and unlimited authority in Heaven and earth, goodness, glory, and divine honors (XIV, 227-237 *passim*), yet the Son is the "image of the glory of his Father" or, like the angels, "clothed in some modification of the divine glory" (XIV, 251). He is one with the Father "in love, in communion, in agreement, in spirit," and he is even entitled to the name of God "by proximity and love" (XIV, 255) and in the capacity of messenger and judge (XIV, 251). The Father communicates divine honors to him (XIV, 303) and invests him with such power that through him the worlds are created (XIV, 323). Here we are interested primarily in the Son's function as minister through whom God creates Heaven and earth. And in creation the Son is ably assisted by the Holy Spirit, also a minister of God, "and therefore a creature . . . created or produced of the substance of God, not by a natural necessity, but by the free will of the agent, probably before the foundations of the world were laid, but later than the Son, and far inferior to him" (XIV, 403). So stands the Son, also called the Word, accompanied by that creature, the Holy Spirit, ready to put into effect designs of the Efficient Cause for the creation of visible and invisible worlds. But no materials have as yet been provided for the grand work.

III

As to the activities of God before creation, the second species of his external efficiency, Milton assures us that "it would be the height of folly to inquire into them, and almost equally so to attempt a solution of the question" (XV, 3). But there can be no doubt that in the process of creation God is revealed as the Primary and Efficient Cause of all things, compassing within himself the hierarchy of all possible causes of whatever kind (XV, 21). Though it is emphasized that "GOD THE FATHER PRODUCED EVERY THING THAT EXISTS BY HIS WORD AND SPIRIT" (XV, 5), there is little evidence to support the theory that he produced matter and chaos, a prepared matter, by such instrumentality.[15] In fact, one might reasonably conclude that matter is an "efflux of the Deity" (XV, 23) directly, at least without any participation of the Son as secondary cause. Here Milton seems to be employing a Neoplatonic concept of emanation somewhat similar to that of Proclus, as I have tried to show elsewhere.[16] But there is this marked difference: for Proclus the emanation of materiality from essentiality of the One is a necessary and eternal process; for Milton the efflux of matter from God occurs at a point of time (XV, 19) and involves the exercise of the divine will.

Now in order to relieve God of all necessity and to maintain the temporal origin of matter, Milton finds it logical to deny the Aristotelian concept of a First Principle "whose essence is actuality."[17] Or as it is developed by St. Thomas, "God is pure act, without any potentiality."[18] In the discussion of omnipotence Milton says: "There seems, therefore, an impropriety in the term of *actus purus*, or the active principle, which Aristotle applies to God, for thus the Deity would have no choice of act, but what he did he would do of necessity, and could do in no other way, which would be inconsistent with his omnipotence and free agency" (XIV, 49). He must postulate, therefore, that before creation—as before generation of the Son—there was in some sense potentiality in God not yet realized in act. Matter cannot have been created out of nothing; emanating from the all-comprehending and all-embracing First Cause, it acquired an external, passive existence in time. Milton continues: "It is an argument of supreme power and goodness, that such diversified, multiform, and inexhaustible virtue should exist and be *substantially* inherent in God (for that virtue cannot be *accidental* which admits of degrees, and of augmentation or remission, according to his pleasure) and that this diversified and substantial virtue should not remain dormant within the Deity, but should be diffused and propagated and extended as far and in such manner as he himself may will" (XV, 21, 23). Here is clearly represented an unactualized substance within God, or rather a power-principle capable of producing substance, which in creation becomes released as matter in actuality. Moreover, this substance-producing power, once idle but now active, admits of degrees, of augmentation or remission, so that, being diversified, multiform, and inexhaustible, it can be diffused, propagated, and extended as far and in such manner as the Deity may will. Could this possibly mean that matter, the substrate of all created things, is a "part" or a diversification of God's essence? If so, Milton cannot escape the charge of being a rank materialist and a pantheist. But as a matter of fact, he is neither. He understands the meaning of substance taken in two senses; he is here only formulating a *suppositum* or postulating a "bodily power" (vis corporea) in the substance of God (substantia Dei), by the exercise of which bodies are emanated from Deity without violence to his numerical unity (XV, 25).

But, like many another philosopher, he cannot answer the perhaps unanswerable question: precisely *how* do material bodies emanate from that Spirit who is God? He supposes that "spirit being the more excellent substance, virtually and eminently [*eminenter*][19] contains within itself the inferior one; as the spiritual and rational faculty contains the corporeal, that is, the sentient and vegetative faculty" (XV, 25). But that bodies do emanate from Spirit he must accept upon faith (XV, 25). His statement, however, that the more excellent substance (i.e., God) "contains" the inferior substance is highly significant. Within limitations of human conceptions and language we may speak of God's "external" efficiency in creation as if he were producing something *outside* of himself and therefore *in addition* to himself. We may even speak of the multitude of "independent essences," or things composed of matter and form, as if they were "independent" of God and were therefore not only "other" but alien creatures. Such necessarily human expressions are misleading. God is infinite; nothing can be added to him or taken away from him; in language contaminated by concepts of space, we may say that his superior substance "contains" all other possible substances. As Milton concludes: "Nor . . . can it be understood in what sense God can properly be called infinite, if he be capable of receiving any accession whatever; which would be the case if anything could exist in the nature of things, which had not first been of God and in God" (XV, 27). Thus even after all creation God "contains" the visible and invisible worlds[20] and is himself uncontained. Consequently, original matter, an efflux of the Deity, "is not to be looked upon as an evil or trivial thing, but as intrinsically good, and the chief productive stock of every subsequent good. It was a substance, and derivable from no other source than from the fountain of every substance, though at first confused and formless, being afterwards adorned and digested into order by the hand of God" (XV, 23).[21] But this ordering and digesting process, evidenced in the creation of Heaven and Hell and the cosmos out of a prepared matter called chaos, is not accomplished by God immediately; it is executed directly by that subordinate person, the Word, aided by that creature, the Holy Spirit.

But let us return to a consideration of undigested and unadorned matter. Milton has just said that "it is only a passive principle, dependent on the Deity, and subservient to him" and that "in number . . . there is no inherent force or efficacy" (XV, 19, 21). It now appears, however, that matter was "confused and formless." One readily understands by the term *formless* that primary matter had not yet been adorned by the accession of substantial forms. But why should the merely passive principle be confused? I shall show[22] how in the *Logic* Milton divides matter into primary and secondary; the secondary into proximate and remote.[23] It is this primary matter which is a merely passive principle and ontologically prior to all its differentiations. The remote-secondary matter is the substance of chaos, which is the substrate of generation and corruption. In chaos prime matter is already differentiated by God into the forms of the four elements—however embryonic or vestigial—or invested with the qualities of the elements, and has acquired quantity and extension. "For," says Milton, "the efficient cause prepares the matter that it may be fit for receiving the form."[24] He is aware, no doubt, of Aristotle's dictum that these "simple" bodies are subject to natural, characteristic, and therefore compelled movements, and that these movements are mutually opposite, one tending upwards and another downwards.[25] And since these elemental bodies have contrarieties in their very nature, it is not surprising to learn that, before the accession of material forms, their movements are in a state of confusion. Milton has this "prepared matter" in mind when he says that it was *confused* and formless, being *afterwards* adorned and digested into order by the hand of God." One gathers that God himself "prepares" the matter directly without the intervention of intermediary causes.

This term *afterwards* (postea) in the above passage suggests that for Milton the order of generative, emanative, and creative processes is of prime importance, involving as it does different concepts of time. As we have seen, the Son was generated in time and before everything else; the Holy Spirit was created at an uncertain point of time, but later than the Son; passive matter was emanated from God in time, reduced to a "confused" prepared matter, and "afterwards" adorned and digested into an orderly creation. Moreover, the Heaven of Heavens, Paradise, and the angels were created at some remote period before the creation of the visible universe in six days (XV, 29, 31, 33, 35). One understands how in the visible world, where bodies move in an emanated space,[26] time should be defined as the measure of their movements, and how God, who is impartible and motionless, should be designated the Eternal. But in what sense can the Word of God and his Holy Spirit, spiritual substances, have been produced in time? The answer to this question follows logically upon Milton's premise that there are potentialities in the substance of God the Efficient Cause. St. Thomas had defended the movement, not only of physical bodies, but also of incorporeal substances[27] and had called the passage of anything from potentiality to actuality another sort of movement.[28] And since "time is nothing else *than the measure of priority and succession in movement,*"[29] it follows that the actualization of potentiality must necessarily be in time. Hence the Son, who had always existed potentially in the bosom of the Father, was generated by decree and so given independent being, necessarily in time; the Holy Spirit was created, i.e., he passed from potentiality to actuality in a movement whose measure is time; and matter is an actualization of an inexhaustible substantial power inherent in God, and this movement must occur in time. But the time-sequence involved in the relation between the production of matter and its accession of material forms has been a mooted question.[30] Suffice it to say that Milton evidently follows such thinkers as Basil, Ambrose, and Chrysostom in holding that the formlessness of original matter preceded *in time* its formation.[31] Hence his statement that matter was *at first* confused and formless and that *afterwards* it was adorned by the hand of God.

IV

Let us grant, then, that God has produced a prepared matter filling all space and that out of this matter the Son and Spirit have "made" or created Heaven of Heavens with its inhabitants, the cosmos, and Hell. In what sense can God be said to exhibit the attribute of omnipresence? This has been called a "very ticklish" question. And Milton, approaching it even with the reverence due Deity, has little explanation of a definite nature to offer. He says under the heading Providence—a species of God's external efficiency—that the Deity "REGARDS, PRESERVES, AND GOVERNS THE WHOLE OF CREATION . . . ACCORDING TO THE CONDITIONS OF HIS DECREE" (XV, 55). That is to say, he "preserves" mankind and all other things "as regards their existence" (XV, 59). Just how the existence of all things is preserved is explained as follows: "His ordinary providence is that whereby he upholds and preserves the immutable order of causes appointed by him in the beginning. This is commonly, and indeed too frequently, described by the name of nature; for nature cannot possibly mean anything but the mysterious power and efficacy of that divine voice which went forth in the beginning, and to which, as to a perpetual command, all things have since paid obedience" (XV, 93). In other words, the Efficient Cause which produced all created things by delegating power and energy to a hierarchy of secondary causes, is still present everywhere in his power and energy as preserver of the original order of causes. Or as John Smith of Cambridge explains it: "The Deity is indeed the Centre of all finite Being, and Entity it self, which is Self-sufficient, must of necessity be the Foundation and Basis of every one of these *weak* Essences, which cannot bear up themselves by any Centrall power of their own."[32] Moreover, just as an earthly king's presence pervades his kingdom in the form of power transmitted through his servants, so the Divine Monarch's governing presence is manifested in the virtue and glory invested in his ministers and messengers. He is present in the Holy Spirit, which sometimes means "the power and virtue of the Father," or that "divine breath or influence by which every thing is created and nourished" (XIV, 359), or "a divine impulse, or light, or voice, or word, transmitted from above through Christ . . . or by some other channel" (XIV, 367), or the "Comforter" (XIV, 373). His ever-present energy is still efficacious in the production of effects outside of the usual order of nature, when he gives the power of producing miraculous effects to whomsoever he may appoint—to the angels, for instance (XV, 95). As the dispenser of his vitality, he is "that *Omnipresent Life* that penetrates and runs through all things, containing and holding it fast together within himself."[33] He is present in all material forms, which are pale reflections, as it were, of the forms or *regula* or ideas in his mind.[34] And as divine intelligence, his omniscience compasses and regards, as in an eternal present, all that has been or can be. John Smith concludes: "and therefore the ancient Philosophy was wont rather to say, that the World was in God, then that God was in the World. He did not look without himself to search for some solid foundation that might bear up this weighty building, but indeed rear'd it up within him, and spread his own Omnipotency under it and through it: and being centrally in every part of it, he governs it according to the prescript of his own unsearchable *Wisdom* and *Goodness*."[35] In this manner Milton might explain the omnipresence of God in the mode of his operational existence.

But Milton has also defined him as being a Spirit, i.e., as an incorporeal substance, or what Neoplatonists would call an intelligible Entity. God must, therefore, be considered as omnipresent according to the mode of his metaphysical subsistence. Milton has little to say on this subject in the *Christian Doctrine*, except to remark that God's substance "contains" all other substances. Indeed, any full explanation of God's spiritual presence in a material world is scarcely possible. For human intelligence, perhaps perceiving incorporeals by intuition but still existing in a world of cor-

poreals, must necessarily be limited in its expression by a
language developed within the confining concepts of extension, space and place, matter and form, magnitude (great
and small), direction (within and without), and duration
of that time which is the measure of movement of bodies.
Still Neoplatonists, such as Plotinus, Porphyry, and others,
have attempted to characterize the incorporeal nature and
to show the relation of the incorporeal to the corporeal. As
Porphyry says, it is so difficult to cognize the intelligible
Being that only vague conceptions of it can be formed.[36]
But this is certain: no properties of the corporeal can be
attributed to it. For example, an intelligible entity or simple
nature—such as Milton's God who is Spirit—is in no sense
subject to ordinary concepts of space and time; it is neither
large nor small—only bodies have mass; it does not occupy
any place, so that the "ubiquity of the incorporeal is not a
local presence."[37] How, then, can God the Intelligible Essence be omnipresent everywhere in the material world?
Commenting upon the figurative sense of the text, "the Lord
came down to see the city," Philo had said: "To suppose
that the Deity approaches or departs, goes down or goes up,
or in general remains stationary or puts Himself in motion,
as particular living creatures do, is an impiety. . . . No, . . .
the lawgiver is applying human terms to the superhuman
God, to help us, his pupils, to learn our lesson. For we all
know that when a person comes down he must leave one
place and occupy another. But God fills all things; He contains but is not contained. To be everywhere and nowhere
is His property and His alone."[38] Plotinus would seem to
agree:

Let us, therefore, contemplate this Divinity who is not present
here, and absent there, but who is everywhere. All those who
have any idea of the divinities admit that they, as well as the

supreme Divinity, are present everywhere. . . . Now, since the
Divinity is everywhere, He is not divided; otherwise, He would
not be present everywhere; He would have His parts, one here,
and another there. He would no longer be a unity; He would
resemble an expanse divided into a number of parts; He would
be annihilated in this division, and all His parts would no longer
form the whole; in short, He would have become body. If that
be impossible, we shall have to admit . . . that the Divinity is
everywhere simultaneously present, entire, and identical.[39]

But it is Porphyry who solves—to his satisfaction—the problem involving the incorporeal Deity's omnipresence in the
corporeal world. The so-called "union" of such entirely different natures cannot be likened to any corporeal operation,
since it is neither a blend, nor a mixture, nor a mere colloca-
tion. The solution of the problem lies in the "assimilation"
of the lower to the higher nature: "The incorporeal is present to the body, not in a local manner, but by assimilation,
so far as the body is capable of being assimilated to the incorporeal, and as the incorporeal can manifest in it."[40]

The Divinity is everywhere because it is nowhere, which
paradox is explained as follows: "All things that possess or
do not possess existence proceed from divinity, and are
within divinity; but the divinity is none of them, nor in any
of them. If the divinity were only present everywhere, it
would be all things, and in all things; but, on the other hand,
it is nowhere; everything, therefore, is begotten in it and by
it, because it is everywhere, but nothing becomes confused
with it, because it is nowhere."[41] Such is the poverty of
human language.

But out of the confusion appear certain comparatively
clear concepts with which Milton would agree. The finite
worlds of creation are emanations "within" the infinity of
God, the incorporeal Being; the Deity as a numerical unity
must be present indivisibly, illocally, and entirely every-

where in everything subject to extension and division.[42] Let us perhaps add to the confusion. Let us cognize God symbolically, as the mystics have done, as an infinity of Light. Now "within" this infinity there is actuated a tiny bubble, as it were, of limited room called space; and within the tiny bubble is actuated the world of created essences. If one should enquire about what is "outside" of the bubble, the answer must be, There is no "outside" of space; there is only an infinite, incorporeal Deity "in" whom all things exist. As Porphyry says, therefore, God cannot *be* all things; the sum of all created essences cannot total God's essence, which is numerically one and infinite. This concept of God's omnipresence in the mode of his metaphysical subsistence may be ultimately incomprehensible, but it cannot be called pantheism. It is a mystical theopantism. We shall see presently how in *Paradise Lost* Milton represents God's omnipresence in this mode.

V

I will not here pursue the idea of God through the whole of *Paradise Lost*. We are not at present concerned with man's first disobedience or with the justification of God's ways to man. But that in the poem Milton represents faithfully the dual concept of the divine nature as formulated in the *Christian Doctrine* cannot be doubted.[43] For example, as metaphysical Being he is pronounced omnipotent, immutable, immortal, and infinite (III, 372-373);[44] "God is light,/ And never but in unapproached light / Dwelt from eternity" (III, 3-5); he is therefore the fountain of light (III, 374). In his unitary perfection no deficiency can be found; he has no need of propagation, "already infinite; / And through all numbers absolute, though one" (VIII, 419-

421). As incorporeal Spirit he is mystically omnipresent—
"for where is not he / Present"? (VII, 517-518). Sending
the Son and Spirit forth into chaos, he remarks, "Boundless
the deep, because I am who fill / Infinitude, nor vacuous
the space" (VII, 168-169); and when the Son returns to sit
by the Father, it is said of the latter, "he also went / Invisible, yet stayed such privilege / Hath omnipresence" (VII,
588-590). Though he is thus omnipresent and always "uncircumscribed," as Creator he cannot according to his nature
involve his immutable essence directly in the process of
creation. He is the unmoved First Principle and as such has
maintained "his holy rest / Through all eternity" (VII, 91-
93). And now that creation is about to be achieved through
secondary causes, he must, as metaphysical Entity, remain
still in his holy rest. As he says, he will "retire"[45] from immediate participation in creation and will not put forth his
creative "goodness" directly (VII, 170-171). Whatever of
the creative complexity can be ascribed to him immediately
—such as the emanation and preparation of matter, the
generation of the Son, and creation of the Spirit—has been
the result of decree or the exercise of purpose; he is not,
like the Neoplatonic One, compelled by necessity. And since
he is indivisible and all-embracing, his divine nature cannot
be subject to any contingencies. As he proclaims, "necessity
and chance / Approach not me" (VII, 172-173). Here the
metaphysical Abstraction begins to take on properties of
the Efficient Cause.

In the manifestation of his excellence and power as Primary Cause of all possible effects, he is the all-powerful
Monarch: "Eternal king; . . . author of all being" (III, 374)
or "invisible king, / Only omniscient" (VII, 122-123) or
"omnipotent / Eternal father" (VII, 136-137). As such, his
free will is naturally emphasized; he himself says that his

creative goodness "is free / To act or not" (VII, 171-172).
It may be recalled that in the *Christian Doctrine* (XIV, 27)
Milton had shown impatience with those who, like some
Neoplatonists,[46] associate fate merely with the workings of
nature, and had concluded, "Fate can be nothing but a divine decree emanating from some almighty power."[47] Accordingly, it is not surprising to hear the Only Omniscient
saying, "and what I will is fate" (VII, 173). Moreover, as
Omnipotent Intelligence he beholds the past, present, and
future (III, 78). He foresees and foretells the perversion of
mankind, endowed by unalterable decree with free will
capable of making choices, and defends his foreknowledge
from the imputation of injustice (III, 80-134). And the
"supreme of heavenly thrones, / First, highest, holiest, best"
(VI, 723-724) is constantly praised by the Son and the angels
for his graciousness and mercy, for the rightness of his judgments, and for his wisdom and truth (III, 144 ff.). So the
Deity is represented in *Paradise Lost* as the Author and
Ruler of all things.

God's Son is also properly represented as a derivative and
therefore secondary person in whom and through whom the
Father manifests his power and glory (III, 63), the "divine similitude, / In whose conspicuous countenance, without cloud / Made visible, the almighty father shines" (III,
384-386). Or, in his most glorious Person "all his father
shone / Substantially expressed" (III, 139-140). Or, as the
Father addresses him:

> Effulgence of my glory, Son beloved,
> Son in whose face invisible is beheld
> Visibly, what by deity I am
> And in whose hand what by decree I do (VI, 680-683).

As might be expected, he is sent forth with the Holy Spirit
to create a new World (VII, 208) answering God's Idea

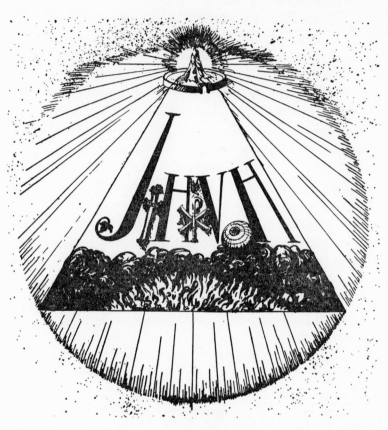

A DIAGRAM INDICATING MILTON'S CONCEPT OF TOTAL
SELF-EXISTENT AND DEPENDENT REALITY OR BEING AS
REPRESENTED IN SYMBOLICAL DESIGN[48]

(VII, 558). Thus the Son, in whom virtue and grace have been "transfused" (VI, 703-704) and on whom "transfused" the Father's "ample spirit rests" (III, 389), is exalted and anointed "universal king" (III, 317), the Father's "word, . . . wisdom, and effectual might" (III, 170), "Vicegerent son" (X, 56), "Second omnipotence" (VI, 684), and in this sense, after incarnation and ascension, "God" (III, 316), "Equal to God, and equally enjoying / God-like fruition" (III, 306). In this same manner, it will be recalled, Milton rationalizes the relationship between Father, Son, and Spirit in the *Christian Doctrine.*

It may be observed briefly, in conclusion, that Milton's philosophical system as developed in the *Christian Doctrine* is reasonably consistent with itself and well constructed. In the *Paradise Lost,* having permitted his interpreting rational faculty to play upon intuited knowledge revealed in Sacred Scriptures, he succeeds admirably in representing God as metaphysical Entity with epic grandeur and sublimity. But one must admit with some reluctance that at times his portrayal of God as arbitrary King and Author of all being is less successful. He finds it necessary, of course, to represent the concrete character of Divinity by the exercise of imagination. But in the process of likening the spiritual to the corporeal, in bodying forth the actions and speeches of God, Milton is sometimes betrayed, it seems to me, into limiting the dramatic effectiveness of the divine Monarch's power and glory. Nevertheless, it must be emphasized again that in both the *Christian Doctrine* and in *Paradise Lost* the philosopher-poet is consistent in his presentation of the fundamentally same dual concept of Deity: God in the mode of his metaphysical subsistence, and God in the mode of his operational existence.[49]

Chapter 2

WHEN SATAN IN MILTON'S PARADISE LOST STRUGGLES through the turmoil of chaos until he approaches the coast of darkness bordering upon light, he meets two Powers or Spirits of the nethermost Abyss, Chaos and ancient Night.

> behold the throne
> Of Chaos, and his dark pavilion spread
> Wide on the wasteful deep; with him enthroned
> Sat sable-vested Night, eldest of things,
> The consort of his reign (II, 959-963).

These ancestors of Nature subsist by virtue of the confusion over which they hold sway: Chaos, the old Anarch, sitting as umpire in the eternal conflict between embryon atoms, by decision more embroils the fray, and eldest Night establishes and maintains her standard upon the tumult and wild disorder of the realm between Heaven and Hell.[1] Thus Milton presents two perplexing figures, two deities, ruling over a wild Abyss represented as being the womb of Nature and perhaps her grave.

MILTON'S CHAOS
AND OLD NIGHT

Comment upon the sources and precise significance of the poet's conception of Chaos and Old Night is usually brief and somewhat hesitant. Indeed, Miss Nicolson concludes: "In *Paradise Lost* we may dismiss as unessential much of the 'myth' of Chaos and Old Night."[2] Professor Osgood finds that "There is . . . little or no classical authority for Chaos as a distinct divinity ruling and maintaining the great region of anarchy and confusion above Hell."[3] He surmises, however, that the conception of Chaos as a ruling god may be traced ultimately to "Hesiod, though his representation is much less definite than Milton's, and amounts to little more than a personification of a condition in the order of nature's earliest development."[4] On the other hand, it is generally conceded that "The Miltonic conception of Night is based upon that of the Orphic cosmogony, which makes her the eldest and first of all things."[5] Such observations are stimulating and, within certain limitations, likely to be correct. But they evidently do not explain fully the sources of the poet's concept of Chaos as a god, or the precise relationship between Old Night and that Orphic Night "From whom at first both gods and men arose,"[6] or why both Chaos and Old Night should be represented as corulers over chaos, or why in some sense they seem hostile to good. Any adequate solution of these problems, it seems to me, requires a consideration not only of ancient cosmogonic myths but also of later theological interpretations of them.

I

Accordingly, this present chapter is designed to defend the hypothesis that the conception of the divinity of both Chaos and Night was in accordance with the doctrines of Neoplatonic theology in its interpretations of Orphic and Pythagorean cosmogony. Specifically, it aims to show that Chaos may be identified with the second divine principle of the "intelligible triad," and Night with the first or summit of the so-called "intelligible and at the same time intellectual triad" of the Neoplatonic system. It suggests also that Milton could easily have found philosophical support for his fusion of these occult Powers—introduced primarily for poetic or dramatic reasons—with a cosmogony which, at first glance, might seem alien to them.

But before the status of a divine Chaos can be precisely defined, it is necessary first to investigate the nature of a profound mystery, the intelligible triad. Neoplatonic theology, as represented especially in the commentaries of Proclus, celebrates the emanation of a multifarious reality from a primary Unity sometimes called "the One" or "the Good." This principle of all things, God, is so ineffable that he is beyond all knowledge and comprehension; he is the first

cause of all causes, the supreme unity of all unities, superessential, transcending all being, the "thrice unknown darkness" to be venerated in silence.[7] As the fountain of all
deity, however, he unfolds himself into light through six
successive and unified stages of activity; or more properly
speaking, he manifests his power through six genera of divine natures: namely, the *intelligible order*, the *intelligible
and at the same time intellectual*, the *intellectual*, the *supermundane*, the *liberated*, and the *mundane*.[8] Here we are at
present interested in only the first order, i.e., the *intelligible*
genus of divine principles, which is logically prior to all other
emanations. It must be observed that, since this order is
nearest of all things to "the One," its union must necessarily
be transcendently profound and ineffably occult; indeed, it
may appear to the eye of our intellect as a single splendor
beaming from an unknown and inaccessible fire. Human
conceptions are so imperfect, however, that for convenience
philosophers assign a triple division to its all-perfect mode
of subsistence and, viewing the order in a distributed way,
speak of it as the *intelligible triad*.[9]

Now, according to the mystic doctrine of Proclus—who
here employs the Platonic terminology—the hypostases of
the intelligible triad are *bound, infinity,* and the *mixture* of
these. Bound and infinity, respectively the first and second
processions from the One, are the divine principles through
which are unfolded first causes into all succeeding orders of
beings and progressions, even to the last things: "bound,
indeed, being the cause of stable, uniform, and connective
deity; but the infinite being the cause of power proceeding
to all things and capable of being multiplied and, in short,
being the leader of every generative distribution. For all
union and wholeness, and communion of beings, and all

divine measures, are suspended from the first, bound; but all division, prolific production and progression into multitude, derive their subsistence from this most principal infinity."[10] These principles transcend being and are superessential. In some measure, as we shall see, they may be considered as analogous to form and matter in the ultimate progression.[11] Now mixture of these two, the third hypostasis of the intelligible triad, is first of all beings and therefore the first intelligible essence. As a whole it derives its subsistence from the One; but from bound it receives elements of stability and uniformity, and from infinity it acquires a generative power which is occultly the source of all progressions into a multitude of beings. It is the One-Many; it is all things occultly and, on this account, is the cause of all beings.[12] We must emphasize the fact, however, that in first natures such as this the Many subsist occultly and without separation, and multitude is concealed and may be defined according to union alone.[13] Thus Proclus would present the divine principles of the intelligible triad; "bound" is an "intelligible God primarily," "infinity" is "an intelligible and intellectual God," and "mixture" of these is "an intellectual God." He concludes: "These three deities . . . give completion to the intelligible genera."[14] This triad considered as a monad is paternal in nature, though fatherhood is inherent mainly in the third hypostasis, which is the first "apparent" god and father of all succeeding wholes.

As the intelligible triad pours its powers out into the subordinate and analogous orders of divine natures, it is necessary to postulate somewhere between the intelligible and intellectual gods a parturient or medial genus called the *intelligible and at the same time intellectual* triad. Of this triad we are here concerned with only the first or summit, denominated by Proclus—following Plato—the *supercelestial place*.[15] In its intellectual aspect this hypostasis is presented as a feminine nature; it is described, positively, as being "truly existing essence," or "essence which truly is," or negatively, as having neither color nor figure. Says Proclus: "The supercelestial place is maternal, subsisting according to infinity, and the power of infinity. For this order is feminine and prolific, and produces all things by intelligible powers. Hence also, Plato calls it a place, as being the receptacle of the paternal causes, and bringing forth, and producing the generative powers of the Gods into the hypostasis of secondary natures."[16] It is the "cause of those things maternally of which the intelligible father is the cause paternally"; it is "the mother and nurse of the Gods" who "not only receives, but also constitutes and generates secondary natures, together with the father." "Nor does this generative deity produce from herself into an external place, her progeny, and separate them from her own comprehension, in the same manner as the natures which generate here, deliver their offspring into light external to themselves; but she generates, comprehends and establishes all things in herself. Hence also she is the place of them, as being a seat which on all sides contains them, and as by her prolific, and primarily efficient powers, preoccupying and containing in herself, all the progressions, multitude and variety of secondary natures."[17] Thus, in the concept of supercelestial place Proclus provides for a union of masculine and feminine principles through which original essences are nurtured and transmitted into all posterior beings. He also conceives here of the procession of power—inherited from infinity—into energy and ultimately into motion. And in supercelestial place he discovers the first manifestation of space, in which the succeeding process of emanation may be consummated.

Let us now observe how late Neoplatonists and others would apply this doctrine of the intelligible triad in their interpretations of the ancient cosmogonies, such as those delivered by Hesiod, Orpheus, and his follower, Pythagoras. Says Damascius, the successor of Proclus: "The theology contained in the Orphic rhapsodies concerning the intelligible Gods is as follows: *Time* is symbolically placed for the one principle of the universe; but *aether* and *chaos*, for the two posterior to this one; and *being*, simply considered, under the symbol of an egg. And this is the first triad of the intelligible Gods."[18] In this manner he would identify the Orphic Time with the One, Aether with bound, the Pythagorean Chaos with infinity, and Being or the celebrated Orphic Egg with mixture.[19] And with this same mixture may be identified also the Orphic Protogonus,[20] sometimes called Ericapaeus and Phanes. Moreover, in accordance with this system Damascius interprets other Orphic traditions which seem to postulate Phanes or a Dragon as the first and original God: "But I likewise find in the Orphic rhapsodies, that neglecting the two first principles [i.e., *Aether* and *Chaos*], together with the one principle who is delivered in silence [i.e., the *One* or *Time*], the third principle, posterior to the two [i.e., *Phanes* or *mixture*], is established by the theology as the original; because this first of all possesses something effable and commensurate to human discourse. For in the former hypothesis, the highly reverenced and undecaying *Time*, the father of aether and chaos, was the [first] principle; but in this *Time* is neglected, and the principle becomes *a dragon* [i.e., *Phanes*]."[21] Proclus himself speaks of a "royal series of the Gods" consisting of Phanes, Night, Heaven, Saturn, Jupiter, and Bacchus.[22] And Syrianus—in his commentary on the fourteenth book of Aristotle's *Metaphysics*—concludes:

Ancient theologists . . . assert that *Night* and *Heaven* reigned, and prior to these the mighty father of Night and Heaven, who distributed the world to Gods and mortals, and who first possessed royal authority, the illustrious Ericapaeus. . . .

Chaos transcends the habitude of sovereign dominion; and with respect to Jupiter, the oracles given him by Night, manifestly call him not the first, but the fifth immortal king of the Gods.

According to these theologists therefore, that principle which is most eminently the first, is the *one* or *the good,* after which according to Pythagoras, are those two principles *Aether* and *Chaos,* which are superior to the possession of sovereign dominion. In the next place succeed the first and occult genera of the Gods, in which first shines forth the father and king of all wholes and whom on this account they call *Phanes.*[23]

In these expositions it is to be observed that not only does the Pythagorean Chaos emerge as the second divinity of the intelligible triad, but feminine Night correctly follows father Phanes or Ericapaeus as the first of the intelligible and at the same time intellectual triad. She is, therefore, to be identified with Proclus' supercelestial place, which is described as being without color or figure.[24] Some writers, indeed, begin the royal series of the gods with this feminine hypostasis. In those writings of the Peripatetic Eudemus containing the theology of Orpheus, for example, the whole intelligible order is passed over in silence, as being in every way ineffable, unknowable, and not subject to verbal expression. Eudemus, therefore, commences his genealogy from Night, the mother of the gods.[25] Eudemus asserts that Homer begins with Ocean and Tethys; but Damascius says,

"It is . . . apparent, that *Night* is according to Homer the greatest divinity, since she is reverenced by Jupiter himself. . . . So that Homer begins his genealogy of the Gods from *Night*."[26]

Other ancient speculations regarding Chaos and Night are brought by Damascius into accord with the Neoplatonic doctrine of the intelligible triad. Acusilaus seems to establish Chaos for the One, and female Night for infinity.[27] And when Hesiod in his *Theogony* asserts that Chaos was first generated with Earth following, Damascius understands that he "signifies by Chaos the incomprehensible and perfectly united nature of that which is intelligible . . . or a certain principle of the whole procession of the Gods." In that case, Chaos may be called the intelligible monad which, considered distributively, is conceived as the intelligible triad.[28] And, says Hesiod, "From Chaos came forth Erebus and black Night."[29]

It will be observed that these interpreters of ancient cosmogonies are not entirely in agreement. But whether Chaos is established as "the One," or as the perfectly united nature of that which is intelligible, or as the second hypostasis of the intelligible triad, he is universally presented as a transcendent god and the active or masculine principle in the procession of other gods. And whether Night is identified with the second hypostasis of the intelligible triad or with the summit of the following order, she is always the goddess and the passive or maternal principle in all progressions even to the last things. In spite of a diversity of opinion in these interpretations, however, we may safely conclude that the Pythagorean Chaos is to be equated with the Neoplatonic infinity, and the Orphic Night with "supercelestial place."

Nor, in accordance with this doctrine, does it matter particularly with which god or divine order we begin our genealogy of the gods. Each hypostasis of the intelligible triad is represented by analogy in every succeeding order. If the One, and Aether, and Chaos—all superessential and beyond being—are too transcendent for our comprehension, we may reverence them in silence and call Phanes or Ericapaeus the first father of all posterior wholes. If essence, being, and intellect in Phanes should prove too occult and unified for our understanding, we may pronounce his successor Night the first of the royal series of divinities. And if the mystery and blackness of Night should defy penetration, we may reverence *Jupiter* in the intellectual order—analogous to Phanes in the intelligible—as the "all-parent, principle and end of all / . . . the first and last."[30] For all the gods and orders of gods subsist in one primary unity, each being in all and all in each.

It may now appear that Milton has some justification for presenting Chaos "the infinite" as a god and for establishing Night, the maternal receptacle and nurse of all generative energies, as a goddess and the copartner of his reign. It is a commonplace among ancient theologists to ascribe to "the One" or God himself a dual nature, or male and female together, signifying mystically thereby the generative or creative power of that first Deity who produces all things from himself alone.[31] It is therefore evident that the female principle must also subsist occultly in the primarily masculine order of intelligibles, because from Phanes comes forth Night, the first apparent expression of the maternal. Further, by analogy, in the intellectual order it is Jupiter, the primarily paternal principle, who is pronounced by the Or-

phic rhapsodist to be "both a man and an immortal maid."[32]
And in the mundane order the Sun through his light preserves an analogy to Phanes, the first father, and the Moon
to Night.[33] And Milton concludes:

> and other suns perhaps
> With their attendant moons thou wilt descry,
> Communicating male and female light,
> Which two great sexes animate the world (*PL.*, VII, 148).

II

It is by no means clear, however, why Milton should pronounce the goddess Night to be the "eldest of things." It
may be, as Osgood suggests, that he bases this concept upon
the Orphic cosmogony, where Night is indeed addressed as
parent Goddess, source of all things, "From whom at first
both Gods and men arose."[34] Or perhaps he is here following the Homeric tradition, reverencing in silence the whole
order of intelligibles and beginning his genealogy of divine
principles from Night. In either case, however, it is difficult
to understand how a sovereign Chaos could be considered,
according to any philosophical interpretation, as posterior to
"eldest Night" and therefore her product or son. Or it is
possible that the poet is here achieving a symbolical association of the goddess Night with the "thrice pronounced darkness" celebrated by the Egyptians as the incomprehensible
first principle of all things,[35] or with the Biblical "darkness
on the face of the deep," or with the Babylonian "darkness"
out of which the universe developed,[36] or with the Hermetic
"downward-tending darkness, terrible and grim" appearing
first upon the face of illimitable Light where the cosmos is

later established.[37] Milton, however, nowhere speaks of Night as first of the gods or as the mother of gods and men; he merely says that she is the eldest of things. No doubt the significant word in this descriptive phrase is *things*. In any true explanation of Old Night, therefore, one might well observe his concept of the nature of things and associate it with the theology of intelligibles presented above.

In the *Art of Logic* Milton notices that what are commonly called individuals or things differ in number among themselves and that whatever things differ in number differ also in essence. "For number, as Scaliger rightly says, is an affection following an essence. Therefore things which differ in number also differ in essence; and never do they differ in number if not in essence. *Here let the Theologians awake.*"[38] Now an awakened theologist such as Proclus, for example, would undoubtedly agree with Milton that essence—respectively *form* in the last progressions—and not matter is what distinguishes one thing from another. But the important question is this: at precisely what stage in the procession of an infinite multitude of things from the unified One are occult principles distributed into individual essences, recognizable as such by the intellect? Proclus has said that the One is superessential; but since he is the cause of all causes, he must have subsisting within himself the "principle" of all essence—as of all other posterior manifestations. Bound and infinity are also pronounced superessential; but bound is the summit or foundation, as it were, of all individual essences, which are nevertheless still concealed in the blinding light of the first procession. It is the *mixture* of bound and infinity which is denominated the "first intelligible essence," because from bound it receives the stable principles of essences. But here, also, as we have seen, the Many subsist occultly and still without recognizable distinction or distribution. "For," says Proclus, "by how much being is nearer to *the one*, by so much more does it conceal multitude, and is defined according to union alone."[39] But when "mixture" or Phanes pours forth intelligible essences and powers into supercelestial place or Night, then complete separation or distribution of essences into a multitude of beings actually takes place for the first time. And for that reason supercelestial place or Night, in her intelligible aspect, is described as being "truly existing essence" or "essence which truly is." Then if things differ in number and individuality in accordance with a difference in essence, Milton is nicely accurate in calling Old Night, the first truly existing essence, the "eldest of things."

III

But why should Chaos and Night, masculine and feminine deities, be represented as ruling over a thoroughly disorganized chaos out of which the sensible universe has been generated? Why should Milton in this manner associate these occult processions from the One with this last or next to the last progression? These questions may find simple answers when we consider further the conception of a degenerating emanation. The emanative process, as elaborated by Proclus, may be fairly represented as a timeless and necessary procession of power and energy from the One into a hierarchy of effects, so arranged that each effect is the product of that which precedes and the necessary generator of that which follows. Though in being thus scattered abroad these powers suffer no diminution, still the effects produced occur in the order of a gradation from the abstract to the concrete. Thus Proclus would postulate a hierarchy of ideas or concepts to which, he believes, corresponds precisely a hierarchy of existences extending from Unity (God, the One), through six successive orders of gods, to the concrete and multifarious phenomena of the visible world.[40] In this emanative process the last order of incorporeal divinities, the mundane gods, extend their generative power into the visible world through their subordinate spirit, Nature, which receives both matter and form ultimately from the One and combines them in varying degrees of perfection.

Conceptually, the ultimate progression in the emanative process is "matter." For Proclus matter is formless and without qualities, simple, invisible; it is, he says, "pure deformity, and the lowest of existent beings as it entirely lacks measure and beauty."[41] Since it is the last manifestation, he must ascribe to it a real subsistence. It is an entity, a being whose very essence is its measurelessness, indefiniteness, incommensurability, and deficiency of power. Its nature, however, is not a positive "removal or privation" of measure, but merely a "lack of measure and limit."[42]

Matter exhibits its own aptitude as subservient to the construction of the whole world, and was from the first produced as the receptacle and, as it were, the mother and nurse of generation.[43] Since, like all other natures, it proceeds from God, it is good; or at least it is neither good nor bad, but necessary only.[44] As it appears in all composite natures, however, it is the contrary of form or reason. And one may arrive at the concept of matter by observing that individual things are subject to deterioration or to evolution toward perfection in proportion as matter dominates form, or vice versa. For all material things suffer naturally through a deficiency of essential power.[45] This power is, as it were, merely a "ray, an impression and reason or form of total Nature, being divided from thence, flowing downward into a body, and incapable of remaining unmingled and pure." Sometimes, as a consequence, "this partial nature weakens, becomes degraded, lets up in its energy, and its emitted light darkens. When reason or form ceases to dominate, passion shames nature, and as its order weakens, the partial natures becomes disordered; its reason becomes vanquished by its subordinate, and itself becomes irrational."[46] And ultimately, in this process of degeneration, there emerges the concept of a final progression so predominantly matter that the power of forms is altogether suppressed; a purely occult existence, not positively deprived of the "rays" of Nature—which would pronounce it nonbeing—but entirely lacking "even the faintest degree of intelligible splendor." Neoplatonists, therefore, identify matter in symbolical language with "darkness."[47] But it is clear that matter nowhere occurs in nature entirely deprived of forms. Since, as Proclus says, matter is all things in capacity, then forms must be occultly suspended in it and must subsist there in pure simplicity without qualities, distinction, or motion.[48] This matter, however, is in no sense a composite body.

Evidently the last composite body—i.e., the next to the last progression—is chaos. This manifestation requires, of course, the material substrate common to all bodily composites. But here forms and potencies have degenerated to the status of mere vestigial elements. And because these vestiges of Nature's "rays" are dissimilar and unbalanced, the composite is represented as subsisting in a state of violent and disorderly motion. Says Proclus: "The first composite . . . with a representation of all forms in itself,—and these, as it were, in a confused state,—in being moved, produces that which is inordinate. For the vestiges of different forms, leading to different local motions, manifest the whole motion to be fluctuating and turbulent."[49] Thus Proclus would identify the last composite body of his emanative process with Plato's first composite body or chaos, out of which the Demiurgus fabricates the cosmos.[50]

Proclus' theology is mystical and no doubt fantastic, but it furnishes a philosophical basis for Milton's association of Chaos and Old Night with those elementary, chaotic materials out of which Heaven, Hell, and cosmos are created. Here it must be emphasized again that the hypostases and organization of the intelligible triad are reproduced by analogy in each of the succeeding orders of divinities. Even in the partial natures of the material world, from the most nearly perfect down to matter itself, these principles of the intelligible genera are represented more or less clearly. And as we have said, the male and female principles are found everywhere operative even to the last manifestation of divine power. We have already identified Chaos with infinity and Old Night with supercelestial place, the female principle which runs analogously through all posterior orders even to the last things. Now in the corporeal world infinity is analogous to matter, and bound to form. "For what else," says Proclus, "is the infinite in body, than matter? and what else is bound in it, than form?"[51] In the last progression, therefore, that occult matter which completely lacks measure and limit is the infinite.[52] In chaos, the last composite body, the material substrate (the infinite) is that which accounts for its measurelessness, for its infinity of capacity, for its violence and turbulence of motion—because here the power of infinity is inadequately restrained—and for its indefiniteness and "blackness." Therefore, the divine Chaos, identified in the above manner with the infinite, is fittingly represented by Milton as ruling over this disordered realm—spreading his dark pavilion wide on the wasteful Deep—and maintaining his reign by virtue of the confusion which he is at pains to foster.

Old Night, as we have seen, is a feminine divinity who is the receptacle of paternal causes, transmitting into all posterior things the generative powers of the gods. In her intelligible aspect, she is the first truly existing essence and the nurse of all essences; in her intellectual capacity, she subsists according to infinity and the power of infinity. In the last progressions, therefore, she also is analogous to matter considered as the mother and nurse of the reasons or productive principles. In chaos or the last composite body, then, she is responsible for the presence of forms if only in a vestigial state and therefore for motion, which is a degeneration as it were of vital power and energy transmitted through her from infinity; she is the place in which extended bodies may exist and the room in which movement of bodies is possible. In chaos she is the infinity of extension—though, as Proclus says, "it is very loosely that we speak of incommensurability, the infinite, and such concepts."[53] Since forms or essences of Nature are here weakened to mere vestiges, she is necessarily irrational and disordered; she is without figure. Or, to use symbolical speech, the rays of light which Nature casts upon matter have here been weakened and darkened almost to the point of extinction, so that she subsists in a "lack" of light, which is darkness.[54] She is sable-vested and without color. She is the Deep considered as extension, the Abyss which is the womb of Nature and perhaps her grave; or as Milton puts it, chaos extended is "the wide womb of uncreated night" (PL., II, 150).[55] In accordance with the Orphic and Neoplatonic theology, therefore, the goddess Night would seem to be by analogy comfortably at home in Milton's chaos. And she is admirably suited to be represented as the consort of that old Anarch, Chaos. For these two divine principles, male and female, are metaphysically so similar and so complexly interrelated that, subsisting by analogy in the last composite body, they are mutually supplemental to the point of being dependent each upon the other for existence.[56]

IV

Why, then, we may ask, should Milton's Chaos and Old Night manifest hostility to the Creation of Heaven and Earth or Hell and seem to applaud the machinations of the malignant Adversary of all good? Any adequate answer to this question necessitates consideration of the origin and quality of evil in the world of composite bodies and its relation to God.

Now in deriving an incorruptible matter from God, Milton is following an ancient and respectable tradition. Diogenes Laertius, for example, reports the opinion of certain Pythagoreans to the effect that "The principle of all things is the monad or unit; arising from this monad the undefined dyad or two serves as material substratum to the monad, which is cause."[57] This dyad may be interpreted as merely "the reason of alterity, inequality, and unconstant irregularity in things";[58] but for most writers the "infinite duality of all things" is to be identified with passive matter upon which the monad as active cause operates.[59] Iamblichus the Neoplatonist ascribes to the Egyptians the concept of mat-

ter's derivation from the pure essence of one first principle.
Says he, "Thus, therefore, the doctrine of the Egyptians concerning principles . . . begins from one principle, and descends to a multitude which is governed by this one. . . .
But God produced matter by dividing materiality from essentiality; and this being vital, the Demiurgus receiving,
fabricated from it the simple and impassive spheres. But he
distributed in an orderly manner the last of it into generable
and corruptible bodies."[60] The Chaldaic oracles also represent all things as springing from one paternal principle or
"central fire"; and upon this concept Psellus comments: "All
things, whether intelligible or sensible, receive their essence
from God alone, and return back again only to him."[61] To
this may be added like testimony of the Orphic hymn:
"Wherefore, together with the universe, were made within
Jupiter the height of the ethereal heaven, the breadth of the
earth and sea, the great ocean, and profound Tartara, the
rivers and fountains, and all other things. . . . Whatsoever
hath been or shall be was once contained in the womb of
Jupiter."[62] But it is Proclus who marshals all available authority in support of his thesis that "Matter too derives from
God, as being necessary to the universe."[63] He affirms that
the Chaldaic and Orphic oracles "deduce or derive matter
from the first hypostasis of intelligibles,"[64] adduces Porphyry's statement that "father is he who generates the universe
from himself,"[65] finds that Plato in *Philebus* produces "matter itself and every nature of the infinite from the one,"[66]
and notes with approval Iamblichus' mystic statement regarding the relationship between essentiality and materiality: "And the tradition of the Egyptians agreeth herewith,
that matter was not unmade or self-existent, but produced
by the Deity: for the divine Iamblichus has recorded, that

Hermes would have materiality to have been produced from essentiality, (that is, the passive principle of matter from the active principle of the Deity:) and it is very probable from hence, that Plato was also of the same opinion concerning matter; viz. because he is supposed to have followed Hermes the Egyptian."[67] Thus the great Neoplatonists, Psellus, Porphyry, Iamblichus, and Proclus agree that matter is an efflux from Deity and that it is, therefore, good and necessary for the creation of the visible world.

Milton, like Proclus and many others, finds it extremely difficult to explain precisely how a material substance flows from the spiritual essence of Divinity. In the *Christian Doctrine* he assumes that there must originally have been "some bodily power in the substance of God" (XV, 25), which produced matter: All things are of God (XV, 21). He observes that "it is an argument of supreme power and goodness, that such diversified, multiform, and inexhaustible virtue should exist and be *substantially* inherent in God . . . and that this diversified and substantial virtue should not remain dormant in Deity, but should be diffused and propagated and extended as far and in such manner as he himself may will" (XV, 21, 23). Or in Neoplatonic terms, the *principle* of materiality is in some way inherent in essentiality, and matter results from the separation of the two. But if you require a more precise definition of the relation between body and spirit, Milton can reply with an analogy only: "spirit being the more excellent substance, virtually and essentially contains within itself the inferior one; as the spiritual and rational faculty contains the corporeal, that is, the sentient and vegetative faculty" (XV, 25). He recognizes that this is a difficult philosophical problem; he finally must rest his solution upon reason and faith. Says he, "Neither is it more incredible that a bodily power should issue from a spiritual substance, than what is spiritual should arise from body; which nevertheless we believe will be the case with our own bodies at the resurrection" (XV, 25). Now Proclus, as we have already seen, postulates a hierarchy of ideas or logical concepts to which, he believes, corresponds a hierarchy of existences, including the phenomena of the visible world. He identifies the principle of materiality—originally inherent in the One—with infinity, the second emanation of the intelligible triad; and it is this hypostasis, as we have observed, which is represented by analogy in the material world as matter. In this manner he would derive material substance from pure spirit. For him the process of derivation is timeless and necessary; for Milton, on the other hand, the process seems to be in time and is certainly directed by God's will.

If Proclus and his followers on down to Milton can affirm that matter is an efflux from God and is therefore good or at least not evil, how can the appearance of evil in the world be explained? Milton says that "it is not true . . . that matter was in its own nature originally imperfect. . . . Matter, like the form and nature of the angels itself, proceeded incorruptible from God; and ever since the fall it remains incorruptible as far as concerns its essence." He states flatly: "Strictly speaking indeed it is neither matter nor form that sins" (XV, 23, 25). And yet, in *Paradise Lost* there is represented a chaos which seems to be largely evil and perhaps in some sense alien to God. Here is discovered the hoary Deep, a dark illimitable ocean, without bound, without dimension, where hot, cold, moist, and dry through endless conflict create eternal anarchy and confusion. Here "Chance governs all" (II, 910); and God says, "necessity and chance /

Approach not me" (VII, 172). Here Chaos and Old Night, apparently God's enemies, further imbroil the fray; and by them stand Rumor, and Chance, Confusion, and Discord with a thousand various mouths. Chaos complains bitterly that his realm has been encroached upon and the scepter of Old Night weakened by the establishment of Hell and, more lately, by the creation of Heaven and Earth out of a portion of the dark Abyss. He would fiercely defend what little is left under his rule. He rejoices in Satan's mission of destruction. "Go, and speed," he urges, "Havoc and spoil and ruin are my gain" (II, 1009-1010). There, where the light from Heaven shoots into the bosom of dim Night a glimmering dawn, is established the outmost works of Nature; and from these defenses the old Anarch retires, "a broked foe / With tumult less and with less hostile din" (II, 1039-1040). But it is significant that he directs no word of enmity against Heaven's King himself. Might not one conclude that chaos, the last composite body in which an incorruptible matter predominates, is for the most part evil and that Chaos and Old Night are without doubt inimical to the organized beauties of Nature and are therefore also evil? The dark materials of chaos can be considered good only in the sense that they are ordained by the Almighty Maker as necessary to his creation of this world and perhaps, if he should so will, of other worlds (II, 915). It would seem, then, that here Milton is convicted of contradiction worse confounded. But in reality the contradiction is only apparent; the poet as usual knows what he is about. He would no doubt explain the predominance of evil in chaos and the hostile spirit of Chaos and Night by reference to the philosophical principle of alterity.

V

Indeed, in the *Christian Doctrine* Milton enunciates, though he does not develop, the doctrine that "otherness" in the world of matter and form is the prime condition of evil. Just after he has declared that neither matter nor form sins, he proceeds: "egressa tamen ex Deo; et alterius facta quid vetat, quin iam mutabilis per ratiocinia Diaboli atque hominis ab ipsis prodeuntia contagionem contrahat et polluatur" (XV, 24). The significant thing here is "et alterius facta . . . iam mutabilis," which Sumner translates as follows: "and yet having proceeded from God, and become in the power of another party, what is there to prevent them, inasmuch as they have now become mutable, from contracting taint and contamination through the enticements of the devil, or those which originate in man himself?" (XV, 25). It is obvious that Sumner's "and become in the power of another party" throws but little light upon the full meaning of "et alterius facta," and Milton nowhere offers further explanation. But it is likely that the poet is here echoing Proclus' celebrated exposition in his work, *On Evil*. Let us, therefore, observe Proclus.

Evil exists in the material realm of composite bodies as a result of two causes.[68] In the first place, we have already observed how, in the process of a degenerating emanation, all partial natures suffer more or less from a deficiency of essential energy and how evil is generated from a privation of symmetry between form and matter. The results of such privation are most apparent in the irrationality of chaos. But more important, evil may also flow from the natural alterity, contrariety, and otherness subsisting between the essences and productive powers inherent in the distributed species of things. It must be emphasized that nothing is contrary to Nature considered as a whole, because from it are derived all natural productive powers. "But to the nature that ranks as a part, one thing is according to, and another is contrary to nature. Thus a lion's form is preternatural to a man's nature, because in man inheres only man's productive power, and not that of any other species. So therefore in every other class of beings the productive powers of different species are different. Hence to a partial nature it pertains . . . to act contrary to nature" (*On Evil*, 33-34). If the action of a partial nature's energy be unobstructed, then everything will proceed naturally, and there will be no place for evil in the world of material bodies and individual beings. But the matter of bodies must sustain all sorts of mutations; and the partial nature may be subject to the dominance of contraries. It is therefore clear that "if a partial nature admit . . . its natural path on one hand, and on the other its contrary which impedes its nature; and if while its reason is one the things different therefrom are infinite,—then indeed have we hit upon its evil" (*On Evil*, 34).

Thus in all of Nature's domain evil may subsist, manifesting itself as conflict between the productive powers of an infinite variety of essences. But it is within chaos, the womb of Nature, that the clash of forces is most pronounced. Here, as we have seen, the vestiges of dissimilar forms, different potencies degenerated to the status of vestigial elements, are in such turbulent battle that evil is rampant. Here the principle of alterity finds its most awe-inspiring application. This so-called evil observed in chaos, however, possesses no independent existence; it subsists only in proportion as it participates of good. For matter and an infinite variety of forms, however poorly or well commingled, are necessary for the creation of the mutable world. This chaos, therefore, while it is sharply distinguished from the organized beauties of the cosmos, is in no sense preternatural to nature. It is a necessary material in Nature's workshop. And the accidental evil of chaos, according with the eternal processes of Nature as a whole, may be called good. So the more or less evil which perpetually surrounds partial natures is absorbed into the perfection of wholes.

Now Milton's Chaos and Old Night, dramatic symbols representing the constitution and function of the last composite body, are evil only in the sense that they war against order in the created universe. In the process of a degenerating emanation, it is their proper office and duty to maintain and rule over disorder; they subsist, as we have seen, by virtue of confusion. They are not "other" than Nature; they are lively personifications of the "originals of Nature" which possess an infinite capacity for being organized into new worlds. The contrariety involved is not that between these deities and Nature but between chaos and creation. Hence that old Anarch, Chaos, naturally laments the recent encroachment upon his kingdom; he would welcome the destruction of Nature's organized and decorated handiwork. Being an ordained constituent of natural processes, however, he reveals no hostility to Nature as such. Satan, indeed, maligns both Chaos and Night by falsely representing them as "Protesting fate supreme" (PL., X, 480). But neither manifests alienation from God; the principle of alterity, with its accompanying evil, applies only in the world of partial natures. Even Chaos and Old Night, embodying a maximum of accidental evil, play a necessary role in the emanative process. They too are assimilated in the uncircumscribed spirit of God.

Thus, philosophically, Milton presents them in *Paradise Lost*. But to the poet's heavenly Muse may be ascribed the rare poetic achievement of investing these divine though abstract powers or principles with quick personality involving the exercise of volition, judgment, and memory, and with the capacity for experiencing the entirely human emotions of joy, hope, disappointment, hesitation, suspicion, and fear. Here, as usual, the primarily creative genius establishes his imaginative structure upon a stable philosophical ground.[69]

Chapter 3

M ILTON'S CHAOS IN PARADISE LOST IS DISORDERLY, BUT
it is palpable and therefore subject to processes of
analysis. Upon proper consideration it is discovered to be a
subsistent entity whose inherent primary qualities, such as
extension, solidity or fluidity, number, and motion, may as
usual be grasped by perception. And these perceived primary qualities have the power of producing a variety of
sensations, secondary qualities such as heat and cold, color,
and sound.[1] It is heterogeneous, a mass of agglomerate materials in various stages of becoming. This chaos in all its
multiplicity of detail is directly prepared by God to serve
as the substrate of all generation and corruption. And underlying the consistence of chaos is that mysterious, passive
matter, an efflux from Deity, which Milton calls "the chief
productive stock of every subsequent good."[2] The present
chapter considers these questions further and concerns itself
also with the various differentiations to which God subjects
passive matter until it becomes a chaos prepared to receive
forms.

THE CONSISTENCE AND
QUALITIES OF CHAOS

Now in Milton's account of the origin of matter he is evidently under the influence of Neoplatonic concepts of emanation. According to this philosophy, as I have shown elsewhere,[3] matter is the last and final progression of a degenerating emanation; it is a purely occult existence produced by a timeless, necessary, and eternal process. For the poet-philosopher, however, the efflux of matter from Deity occurs at a point of time (*DC.*, XV, 18, 22) and involves the exercise of divine will. And having derived matter directly from God, he proceeds—with apparently no consciousness of philosophical contradiction—to consider it the *first* step in the processes of an historical creation. For him it is a purely passive principle or substance, having no inherent force or power but capable of "receiving passively the exertion of divine efficacy" (*DC.*, XV, 19).

One gathers that the first result of God's exertion of efficacy upon passive matter is the differentiation of its indeterminate substance into individual particles called atoms.

In *Paradise Lost* Milton represents graphically the embryon atoms as Satan perceives them moving in the profound void or vacuum. In their several clans some are light, some heavy, some sharp, some smooth, and in motion some are swift, some slow (II, 901-902). They "Swarm populous, unnumbered as the sands / Of Barca or Cyrene's torrid soil" (II, 903-904). And that they flit about in all directions in a "void immense" cannot be doubted (II, 828). For when Satan plunges into the "hoary deep" (II, 891)—a "void" and hyperbolical "formless infinite" (III, 12)—he drops into a "vast vacuity" (II, 932) "Ten thousand fathoms deep" (II, 934).

> and to this hour
> Down had been falling, had not by ill chance
> The strong rebuff of some tumultuous cloud
> Instinct with fire and nitre hurried him
> As many miles aloft (II, 935-938).

And all manifestations in chaos, before creation of the World, may be attributed ultimately to the qualities of these embryon atoms, moving as they do in a void and combining by chance—"Chance governs all" (II, 910)—into ever-changing agglomeration or aggregation of like to like.

Here the poet is evidently indebted in some measure to Democritus, the atomist, or to some seventeenth-century popularizer of Democritean principles.[4] For Democritus[5] too postulates an infinite void or vacuum, in which an infinite number of material particles swarm about in all directions. To these atoms he attributes an unimaginable multiplicity of size and shape together with indestructibility, unchangeableness, and impenetrability. In shape some are rounded or smooth, some sharp or pointed, some provided with "hooks and eyes, with balls and sockets, with involuted

edges, with mortice and dovetail."[6] Their motion is inherent
and eternal; in combination of like to like some move more
slowly than others. For example, in earthy aggregations the
particles are comparatively large and of little mobility; ether
is composed of smaller and rounded particles of fiery swift-
ness.[7] And thus watery particles occasionally meet and
adhere to watery particles, airy particles adhere by chance
to airy, and so on, until agglomerations of atoms, moving in
vortices, and "severing themselves from the infinite vacuum,
they finally become a separate world or cosmos, of which
there are infinitely many."[8]

Resemblances of Milton's atoms to those of Democritus
are evident. Differences are also apparent and significant.
The poet, while postulating a void or vacuum, attributes to
it merely an hyperbolical infinitude; for him only God is
infinite. His atoms embody a variety of motions, but such
motions are not inherently eternal; motion of all particles
derives in time from an immovable Deity. He would not
agree that fortuitous agglomerations of atoms might ultimately produce by chance an infinite number of worlds; for
such an end the application of God's power is necessary.
He would no doubt have supported the statement of his
younger contemporary, the atomist Robert Boyle: "God . . .
having resolved before the creation to make such a world
as this of ours, did divide (at least if he did not create it
incoherent) that matter which he had provided into innumerable multitudes of variously figured corpuscles, and
both connected those particles into such textures or particular bodies, and placed them in such situations and put them
into such motions, that . . . the phenomena which he intended should appear in the universe."[9] Having safeguarded
the proper relationship between Deity and his creation, Mil-

ton levies upon Democritus—and perhaps to some extent upon Epicurus and Lucretius[10]—for such principles of atomistic philosophy as might aid in the execution of his artistic purpose.

What, then, is the origin of the four elements and how do they function in God's differentiation of prime matter into chaos? Democritus assumes, as we have seen, that the primary masses are indivisible and infinite in number and that all things are generated by their agglomeration and involution. Accordingly, air, earth, water, and fire are differentiated by the relative sizes, shapes, and motions of their respective atoms in combinations.[11] Aristotle, of course, opposes this view. He reduces all bodies to the primary constituents or "simple bodies," earth and fire, with the intermediates, water and air[12] and shows how, because of their dual qualities, they suffer a cyclic transmutation one into another.[13] But Lucretius observes that Aristotle's "simple bodies" cannot be considered "first beginnings" because they are said to undergo transmutation; there must be something which remains unchanged. "Why not rather hold," says he, "that certain particles endowed with changeless nature have perchance begotten fire, but also, by addition or subtraction of a few or by a change of motion or of order, can produce the breezes of the air, and that all things can thus be changed, the one into the other?"[14] Thus he would seem to approve the action of the Aristotelian four elements *after they have been generated out of unchangeable first beginnings, the atoms.*

Now with regard to the origin of the four elements, Milton still adheres to atomistic principles. As Satan stands in Hellmouth—which casts forth smoke and ruddy flame—in sudden view there appear before his eyes secrets of the hoary Deep. And one of the secrets which he perceives is the momentary formation of elemental qualities out of embryon atoms:

> For hot, cold, moist, and dry, four champions fierce
> Strive here for mastery, and to battle bring
> Their embryon atoms; they around the flag
> Of each his faction, in their several clans,
> Light-armed or heavy, sharp, smooth, swift or slow,
> Swarm populous, unnumbered as the sands
> Of Barca or Cyrene's torrid soil . . .
>   To whom these most adhere,
> He rules a moment (II, 898-907).

Here is dramatically represented the production of elemental qualities by transitory formation of atoms. Still all is confusion, conflict, and rapid alteration. In this womb of Nature there is as yet neither definite sea, nor shore, nor air, nor fire, "But all these in their pregnant causes mixed" (II, 911-913). The "crude consistence" of primeval chaos which Satan meets later in his flight, however, would indicate that the qualities of hot, cold, moist, and dry are being properly represented in the momently changing forms of earth, water, air, and fire. Thus, as Milton says, the four elements as here conceived are "the eldest birth / Of nature's womb" (V, 180-181). When stabilized and directed by God's power in creation, they behave much as do Aristotle's "simple bodies"; contrarieties in their nature are controlled and they suffer normal cyclic transmutation one into another: "in quaternion run / Perpetual circle, multiform; and mix / And nourish all things" (V, 181-183). But in chaos they are still unstable, uncontrolled, constantly fluctuating in atomic content and in form, energizing confusedly with "fierce extremes" (VII, 272) of heat and cold, wet and dry, in perpetual warfare. Such is the constitution of chaos. It is an actual entity representing the differentiation by God of primary matter into (1) a multitude of atoms and (2) the qualities and changing forms of the four elements. It may logically be identified with that remote secondary matter which, says Milton, the Deity has prepared for the reception of forms in creation.[15]

II

But let us consider further the fluctuating texture or, more properly speaking, the crude consistence and qualities of chaos. It may be perceived as an amorphous mass of momentarily agglomerated atoms and rapidly shifting elemental qualities conceived by the poet to serve a variety of epic purposes. It must furnish materials for the creation of Heaven, Hell, the Mundane Universe, and any other worlds which God may design; its consistence must be of such a nature as to permit Satan's flight through and over it and facilitate the construction of a symbolical highway, following Satan's track, from Hell to the outside shell of the World; and rebellious angels in Heaven tap its crude resources in manufacturing engines of war. One may sense its temporary solidity or fluidity or vacuity, its tremendous extension, and its wild motion. And its heterogeneous contents produce varying pressures of a palpable nature, such as noises which stun the ear and at least one color which distresses the eye.

In Satan's journey through the "illimitable ocean" of chaos, for example, momentary agglomerations of "earthy" particles packed together with only small void spaces between enable him to walk or run upon a density resembling soil,

sometimes rough, sometimes steep. At other times aggregations of "watery" atoms permit him to swim and of "airy"
particles to fly through straits between the dense and the
rare. Sometimes he meets combinations of these earthy and
watery particles in such proportions as to result in what
seems to be bogs and quicksands—neither sea nor good dry
land—over which he must pass, half on foot, half flying.
And once a "cloud" of fiery atoms in contact with the elemental quality of niter causes an explosion which hurls his
body ten thousand miles aloft (II, 936 ff.). Sin and Death
also seem to find this consistence of chaos tractable. When
they start to build their broad way from Hell to the World,
they discover the "illimitable ocean" to be a waste of "waters."[16] They fly out from Hell and gather whatever of
"solid" or "slimy" agglomerations they can find tossed up
and down as in a raging sea and crowd them to Hellmouth.
There Death, with his cold and dry mace, dehydrates and
petrifies the aggregated soil and so fixes it firmly; other
elemental materials he binds with his Gorgonian look and
with "asphaltic slime" not to move (X, 281-298). By this
same process, no doubt, they overbuild disparted chaos with
"bars" (X, 417), construct a bridge of "pendant rock" over
the vexed Abyss, and attach it to the outside shell of the
World with pins and chains of "adamant" (X, 319).

It must be observed that in the representation of this road
from Hell to the World and the process of its construction,
Milton appears to involve himself in artistic and logical
difficulties or perhaps absurdities. The problems are pain-
fully evident: two *allegorical* figures, Sin and Death, are
depicted as building a *symbolical* road composed of such
materials as "bars," "asphalt," and "rock" through an actual
entity, the unformed mass of chaos, to the point where the

symbolical bridge is attached to the outside shell of the created World by chains of "adamant." While Sin and Death may be imaginatively acceptable as personifications of abstract forces or powers, the materials—bars, asphalt, and adamant—in which they are said to energize are as such not native to chaos. Building materials of this nature are actualized products of God's creation of the Mundane Universe, where they may be found in abundance. In the created World of matter and form it is true that a material object—rock, asphalt, bars, a rose—can in the hands of an artist be made to symbolize spiritual or invisible or intangible realities, but the object must itself exist in accordance with the laws of its nature. That is to say, in symbolical representation a rock must be a rock situated in its normal or logical frame of reference, whatever hidden meaning may be imaginatively conceived or attached to it. But in Milton's chaos—whose consistence we have examined—it is not that the highway is, as Dr. Johnson thought, "a work too bulky for ideal architects,"[17] but that it is symbolically defective because the basic terms of the symbol—bars, adamant, rock—represent impossible existences in the chaos frame of reference. In chaos there are discoverable no such actualized building materials.

But perhaps the artistic situation here is not so desperate as it might at first appear. Milton is the epic poet who sometimes sacrifices logical consistency in favor of psychological effect. He evidently depends upon the knowledge of an informed reader that bars, rock, and adamant do exist *potentially* in chaos, else God could not have actualized them in the created World. Consequently, being intimately acquainted with these proximate secondary materials at hand in the Visible Universe, one willingly suspends his logical judgment for a moment and accepts bars, rock, and adamant as basic terms of the highway-symbol. This acceptance is facilitated by recognition of the powers and qualities embodied in the allegorical figures, Sin and Death. They are repulsive forces inimical to mankind. Everybody knows that death is "hungry as the grave" and cold as interstellar spaces; death is a horrible violence and a dryness which, like sorrow, "drinks our blood." Facing these mysteries, one is not surprised when Death strikes unstable materials of chaos with his cold and dry mace so that they are made solid as stone nor when his Gorgonian look reduces chaotically moving "waters" to rigidity (X, 293-297). These are such awe-inspiring images revealing profound truth about the violence and chill of death, that we are willing to grant the poet his "stable" building materials—even in chaos—for the construction of a massive road from Hell to the World. Besides, as we shall see,[18] the definitely limned highway serves admirably to fix directions, perspectives, and distances involved in Satan's journey from Hellmouth to Earth.[19]

That Light which floods the heavenly regions, however, is no mere symbol. It is here, as in the World,[20] the visible manifestation of creative power exercised by the Filial Godhead. The Son, energizing in the Father, has created the Heaven of Heavens (III, 390) and all its inhabiting hosts of angels (V, 837). Satan recognizes that the ethereal and ambrosial beauties of the celestial landscape are created out of the dark materials of chaos by the tempering "Heaven's ray" and that they continue to be so sustained, shooting forth and "opening to the ambient light" (VI, 472-481). It is this same creative Light which, streaming from the battlements of Heaven, shoots a glimmering dawn far into the bosom of contiguous chaos and reduces to some extent its surface instability and disorderly becoming. For here Satan finds in his upward flight that under the creative influence of light—though he must still suffer for a time the shock of well-developed "fighting elements" (II, 1015)—Nature actually begins her farthest verge and chaos to retire (II, 1038). He wafts "on a calmer wave" for a while; and when he finally emerges fully into the precincts of light, he calmly spreads his wings in an atmosphere resembling air (II, 1041-1045). Thus creative light has beaten down chaos into a sort of turbulent sea-surface[21] and has aggregated and ordered airy elements into a calm atmosphere. And this atmosphere is indeed air. God observes the Fiend coasting along the walls of Heaven "in the dun air sublime" (III, 72). Later Satan arrives on the outer shell of the World—hanging "Uncertain which in ocean or in air" (III, 76)—where he walks through the "glimmering air" (III, 429) and is buffeted by storms of this "windy sea of land" (III, 440). It is evident and in no sense surprising, then, that under the sacred influence of creative Light there has been a partial "creation," i.e., a real separation out of chaotic materials of airy particles and qualities and their stabilization into air.

III

One of the most striking qualities of Milton's chaos is its darkness. For example, when the secrets of the hoary Deep are spread before Satan's eyes, he sees it as "a dark / Illimitable ocean" (II, 891-892); Sin and Death are said to discover building materials in the "anarchy of chaos, damp and dark" (X, 283); Satan views the bridge which they have constructed over the "dark Abyss" (X, 371); and when the King of Glory comes with his powerful Word and Spirit to create the World, it is said "On heavenly ground they stood, and from the shore / They viewed the vast immeasurable abyss, / Outrageous as a sea, dark, wasteful, wild" (VII, 210-212). This darkness to which the eye is sensitive is also a tactile quality, i.e., it is capable of being touched or felt. At least Satan wonders who will "tempt with wandering feet / The dark ... abyss" and find a way "through the palpable[22] obscure" (II, 405-406). The poet is aware, of course, that day and night in the created World are both "unsubstantial" and that darkness is "Privation mere of light and absent day."[23] But concerning the original darkness of chaos out of which God caused the light to shine, he says, "That this darkness was far from being a mere negation or nothing, is clear from Isa. XLV.7. 'I am Jehovah; I form the light, and create darkness'" (DC., XV, 17). There can be no doubt that this primordial darkness is to be considered a positive existence created by God when he prepared passive matter for the reception of forms. It resembles in some measure the Democritean *black* and, like that one of the four primary colors, is the effect of aggregations of atoms.[24]

Occasionally, indeed, Milton raises it to the dignity of an allegorical figure, a fierce female personality informing a realm opposed to light and life. For example, the outer shell of the World divides the luminous interior from chaos and the "inroad of darkness old" (III, 421); Adam explains to Eve how light from the celestial spheres exerts a beneficent influence, "Lest total darkness should by night regain / Her old possession, and extinguish life / In nature and all things" (IV, 665-667). Satan conceives that he may perhaps be able to reduce the created World "To her original darkness," "and once more / Erect the standard there of ancient night" (II, 984-985). Or sometimes darkness is identified with the realm itself. Satan returns to Hell "through darkness" (X, 394); the poet is in imagination borne "Through utter and middle darkness" (III, 16); and Satan inquires which way lies "the nearest coast of darkness" bordering upon the realm of light (II, 958). Here one may discern some dim reflection, perhaps, of the Manichaean conception of two territories bordering one upon the other, the Kingdom of Light and the Kingdom of Darkness, sometimes personified and so identified with their rulers.[25] Or perhaps all qualities of primordial darkness may be symbolized by that mysterious "divinity," Old Night. I have already tried to show how and in what sense this female "ruler" serves symbolically as the mother and nurse of all productive principles, the source of motion in chaos, the place in which bodies may exist and the room in which movement of bodies is possible; she is the Deep considered as extension, the Abyss which is the womb of Nature and perhaps her grave. She is sable-vested. With her consort, Chaos, she spreads her pavilion upon the wasteful Deep and erects her standard upon its dark materials.[26]

Still another quality which distinguishes Milton's chaos from most others is its greatly emphasized noise. Here the conflicting particles assail the ear and produce the sensation interpreted as sound. And the noises so sensed are tremendous and unpleasant to the point of being painful. For example, as Satan looks upon chaos, he understands that the confusion there is accompanied by "the noise / Of endless wars" (II, 896).

                    Nor was his ear less pealed
With noises loud and ruinous (to compare
Great things with small) than when Bellona storms,
With all her battering engines bent to rase
Some capital city; or less than if this frame
Of heaven were falling, and these elements
In mutiny had from her axle torn
The steadfast earth (II, 920-927).

As he fights his way through the dark illimitable ocean,

At length a universal hubbub wild
Of stunning sounds and voices all confused
Borne through the hollow dark assaults his ear
With loudest vehemence (II, 951-954).[27]

It is not clear to me where Milton might have found precedent for the inclusion of this vivid quality in his chaos. Genesis mentions no sound in the process of creation. Du Bartas, one of his supposed sources,[28] describes the war between hot and cold, blunt and sharp particles in chaos as "this brawl,"[29] which suggests noisy conflict. In the *Poimandres* of Hermes Trismegistus there is represented at creation a "downward-tending darkness," *amorphos hyle,* which presently changes into a watery substance; "and," says the speaker, "I heard it making an indescribable sound of lamentation; for there was sent forth from it an inarticulate cry."[30] Or perhaps he is transferring the idea of auditory detail found in Biblical descriptions of "last things"—for example, in Luke 21:25, where one hears of "the sea and the waves roaring"—back to his description of "first things."[31] But the establishment of a precedent is really not necessary. Milton is unusually original in his conception of chaos. And since his imagination is largely auditory, he properly and logically associates the conflict between forces in chaos with the naturally resulting noises.

Two further properties of that space or void in which chaos exists and of which it partakes must be considered: namely, dimension and direction. Satan observes chaos as

> a dark
> Illimitable ocean without bound,
> Without dimension, where length, breadth, and height,
> And time and place are lost (II, 891-894).

In order to understand such a statement as this, one must remember that Milton thinks of chaos as originally filling all space, but for him the global space-continuum is only an hyperbolical infinitude existing in an infinity of Light which is God.[32] That is to say, he has in imagination expanded space to such tremendous dimension that it is immeasurable and illimitable. And the chaos which originally filled it partakes of the same quality of extension. Even that part of chaos which remains after creation of three universes—Heaven, Hell, and the World—is still thought of as being immeasurable and illimitable. But within any given portion of it—for example, that part which is visible to Satan—there can be no real dimension because its agglomerations are in a state of kaleidoscopic change and alteration. No aggregation of particles and elemental qualities is of such stability for more than an instant as to suggest that it is capable of being measured with respect to its length, breadth, and height. One may conceive of momentary dense or rare agglomerations, but they have no fixed aggregated parts which might produce measurable shapes and proportions. Interchange of aggregation and dissolution of particles is so rapid that there is produced no such thing as a "body" which can be said to occupy a definite *place* in the void. And the movements of such agglomerations are so erratic and fluctuating that they cannot be measured in terms of *time*. The imaginative poet is admirably effective and accurate, therefore, in suggesting the inconceivable confusion of chaos, where dimension—length, breadth, and height—time and place are lost.

Physicists would agree, I suppose, that direction is a quality of space. And by reason of this property when two positions are known, others may be determined in the like dimension. Mathematically speaking, there is no up and down in infinite space or indeed in the hyperbolical infinitude of Milton's void. As Epicurus says: "Furthermore, in the infinite we must not speak of 'up' and 'down,' as though with reference to an absolute highest and lowest—and indeed we must say that, though it is possible to proceed to infinity in the direction above our heads from wherever we take our stand, the absolute highest point will never appear to us—nor yet can that which passes beneath the point thought of to infinity be at the same time both up and down in reference to the same thing."[33] Still Epicurus would no doubt agree with Lucretius that in infinite space atoms do fall "downward" until a "swerve" in motion causes collision and rebound in all directions. He would recognize that conception of space is relative as well as infinite and that we can think of up and down "with reference to ourselves or to any point in space of which we choose to think. The motion from our feet to our head, however prolonged, is to us motion upward and the opposite motion downwards."[34] It is this concept of space as relative as well as infinite which enables Milton to give direction to movements of individuals in and over chaos. As a matter of fact, two points of reference have already been established for him by convention and authority: Heaven is "above" us, and Hell is "below." It is from this Heaven above that the rebellious angels are cast out, and they fall downward through chaos to Hell below. Satan ascends as in a cloudy chair from Hellmouth into chaos, falls downward in vacuity ten thousand fathoms, is hurled by an explosion as many miles aloft, fights his way upward through chaos and its warring elements until he arrives in the precincts of light off the coast of Heaven, and then pursues a horizontal flight—in relation to the walls of Heaven—over the turbulent sea of chaos southward to the outside shell of the World.[35] So Milton develops that property of space called direction in space-filling chaos.

Analysis of Milton's chaos reveals a remarkable originality of conception and clarity of execution. In his representation of chaotic materials he is attempting, Verity says, "to convey to the reader an impression of utter confusion of the scene described: heaping image on image, idea on idea, by which the imagination may be baffled . . . and the mind bewildered with an insistent sense of the inconceivable."[36] This may be true, but it does not mean that Milton's thinking and feeling are in any sense chaotic. In the bodying forth of his grand chaotic vision he must, as epic poet, necessarily resort to the use of mystic symbol and allegory or other appropriate imagery. To interpreters these may well seem bewildering or baffling; sometimes, as Bunyan says, "metaphors make us blind." But the poet's own imagination is evidently unclouded, his perception sensitive and clear, and his general design carefully delineated. Selecting quite diversified materials from a variety of philosophical and traditional sources, he has syncretized them into a consistent chaos which is completely like no other but which is admirably adapted to his epic design. The consistence of this unique production facilitates dramatic action; its qualities, cleanly defined and related to consistence, are necessary ingredients in all subsequent creations. It is indeed "The womb of Nature, and perhaps her grave."[37]

Chapter 4

REPORTS OF URIEL AND RAPHAEL IN MILTON'S PARA-*dise Lost* on the genesis of a new World are respectively fragmentary, sometimes hazy, and, except by implication, incomplete. Being under the influence of the Jewish tradition, these angels agree of course that God in some manner created the material Universe. But their accounts of an ordered process of creation, stage by stage from a portion of a divinely prepared chaos to the marvelous result, are complicated and confused by the introduction of elements taken apparently from Stoic, rabbinical, Neoplatonic, and atomistic philosophy. It is true that the account in *Genesis* is disconcertingly meager and cryptic enough, seeming to demand amplification: God created the heaven and the earth; the earth was without form and void, darkness was upon the face of the deep, and the Spirit of God moved upon the face of the waters; God said, "Let there be light," and there was light; God said, "Let there be a firmament in the midst of the waters," and the firmament divided the

THE GENESIS
OF MILTON'S WORLD

water from the waters; and so on through the fourth day when the Sun, Moon, and stars appeared to the sixth day when man was created. Both Uriel and Raphael accept the challenge and present such interpretations and amplifications as may be in accord with their individual reactions to the unfolding pattern and spectacle. It is the purpose of this chapter to examine their fragmentary and respectively incomplete reports, to conciliate them if possible, and to reduce to some definite order the progress of creation from chaos to the completed World.

I

Uriel seems to be largely a pious but not too perceptive physicist with inclinations toward atomistic philosophy. He is no doubt thoroughly acquainted with the atomic texture and qualities of chaos[1] and, as close observer, is impressed by the grand spectacle of the evolving World as it develops from a confined mass of chaotic materials to its final perfection. This Regent of the Sun, "The Sharpest-sighted Spirit of all in Heaven," addresses the "stripling Cherub"— disguised but unrecognized Satan, who has recently escaped from shifting agglomerations of elementary particles in chaos—with the significant "I saw":

> I saw when at his word the formless mass,
> This world's material mold, came to a heap:
> Confusion heard his voice, and wild uproar
> Stood ruled, stood vast infinitude confined;
> Till at his second bidding darkness fled,
> Light shone, and order from disorder sprung:
> Swift to their several quarters hastened then
> The cumbrous elements, earth, flood, air, fire,
> And this ethereal quintessence of heaven
> Flew upward, spirited with various forms,
> That rolled orbicular, and turned to stars
> Numberless, as thou seest, and how they move;
> Each had his place appointed, each his course,
> The rest in circuit walls this universe (III, 708-721).

According to this brief sketch a mass of turbulent chaos is first reduced—by God's word—to a global form and its materials brought to a heap. That is to say, the confusion hears God's voice, uproar stands ruled, and hyperbolical infinitude is confined. At God's second command, Light shines, displacing darkness and reducing disorder to order. In this process of bringing order from disorder, like atoms are joined to like in the formation of the four primary elements, which hasten to their several places in hierarchical order, earth, flood, air, and fire. Then ether, the sublimation or quintessence of the four cumbrous elements,[2] springs upward and is formed into the stars, numberless, each rolling orbicular in its appointed course. The remaining ether then is formed into the outer wall of this mundane Universe.

Uriel's account of World-genesis is in some respects similar to that of the ancient atomists. For example, he sees the formless mass, the World's material mold, come to a "heap." Now the word *heap* is in meaning disjunctive, implying a pile or collection of individual and disjoined things thrown or laid together. Milton regularly uses the word in that sense: he speaks of the smutty grains of "a heap of nitrous powder" (IV, 815), "on a heap / Chariot and charioteer lay overturned" (VI, 389-390), "dire hail . . . gathers heap" (II, 589-590), "magic structures . . . shattered into heaps" (*Comus*, 798). Evidently, then, Uriel means that the original, circumscribed mass of chaotic material is a pile or heap of atoms or perhaps momentary conglomerations of atoms. Epicurus agrees that "A world is a circumscribed portion of sky . . . a piece cut off from the infinite and ends in a boundary either rare or dense, either revolving or stationary; its outline may be spherical."[3]

He goes on to say that "worlds . . . were created from the infinite, and that all such things, greater and less alike, were separated off from individual agglomerations of matter."[4] Lucretius also is concerned with the order in which the "confluence of matter founded earth and heaven, the abysses of the sea, the orbits of the sun and moon."[5] He describes vividly how the "first-beginnings," i.e., the atoms, "being numerous and stirred by blows from time now infinite, since they are wont to move, incited by their weights, to make all kinds of unions and try all possible creations by combining with each other, so it is that, sent abroad through many ages, after making trial of all kinds of union and motion, those at length unite which, suddenly combining, oft become beginnings of great things, of earth and sea and sky."[6]

This account of the confluence of atoms into an agglomerated mole of chaotic materials might well serve as amplification of Uriel's vision of the formless mass, the World's material mold, as it came to a heap. The enthusiastic Archangel further elaborates his concept by observing that the confusion and uproar of a portion of general chaos, hearing God's voice, stood ruled to the extent of its being confined and limited within the form of an hyperbolically infinite sphere. Thus, for Uriel this first spectacle in the process of World-genesis is staged by the word of God; but for Lucretius, it is the result of haphazard arrangement of particles without any exercise of sagacity or design.[7]

But within the global mass no order has as yet been achieved. Consequently, Uriel proceeds to the second step in the process of creation. No doubt remembering *Genesis* and God's second bidding, he is made to see how that darkness which was upon the face of the Deep is put to flight by the appearance of Light. He does not say that this Light is really the creative force operative in all subsequent developments—which he must know to be true; he merely proclaims, with a grand sweep of imaginative rhetoric, "Darkness fled, Light shone, and order from disorder sprung." J. A. Comenius, seventeenth-century educator and atomic physicist, informs us in some detail regarding the nature of Light and its function in World-genesis. Having postulated that the *"matter of all the elements . . . is made up of Atomes,"*[8] he formulates six aphorisms concerning Light:

I. *The first light was nothing else but brightness, or a great flame, sent into the dark matter to make it visible and divisible into form.*

II. *God put into the light a threefold vertue: 1 of spreading itself every way, and illuminating all things. 2 of moving the matter with it being taken hold of, by burning and inflaming. 3 of heating, and thereby rarifying and attenuating the matter.*

III. *But when as that light could not extend his motion upwards and downwards . . . it moved itself, and doth still move in a round: whence came the beginning of dayes.*

IV. *And because the matter rarified above heat being raised by the motion of the light, the grosser parts of the matter were compelled to fall downward, and to conglobate themselves in the middest of the Universe: which was the beginning of the earth and water.*

V. *The light therefore by its threefold vertue, light, motion, and heat) introduced contrariety into the World.* For darkness was opposite to light; rest, to motion; cold, to heat.

VI. For the light is the onely fountain both of visibility, and of motion, and of heat. take light out of the World, and all things will return to *Chaos.*[9]

Now Uriel might well agree with some such analysis of Light's nature and function. But in his haste he ignores or skips over some of the most important Light-activities—for example, heating of the mass—or is content to include them all in "order from disorder sprung." Being Regent of the Sun, he is naturally interested in illumination and in that motion which involves the formation and separation of the four elements, the upward flight of ether, and in the creation of planets and stars rolling in their courses.

But the Sun's Regent, illustrating the emergence of order from disorder, is curiously silent on just how the four cumbrous elements—earth, flood, air, and fire—are differentiated from the atomic mass, to what definite "quarters" they are said to have "hastened," and on what may be the relationship between the "ethereal quintessence of Heaven" and the four elements. He merely arranges elements and ether in hierarchical order, which may or may not be the sequence-order of their differentiation. Perhaps the atomic physicists can furnish some enlightenment on these questions. On formation of the elements, Democritus, for example, assumes that earth, water, air, and fire are differentiated in accordance with the sizes, shapes, and motions of atoms in combination.[10] Lucretius observes that "each thing's particles are all distributed to it by blows from every quarter, and they go apart, each to its proper kind; moisture to moisture moves; from earthy particles grows earth; fire forges fire and ether ether."[11] Uriel must have seen this process in momentary operation even in primeval chaos,[12] but he disregards it here. No doubt most early cosmogonists would approve of the angel's hierarchical arrangement of elements and ether in the completed Universe. But in what sequence-order were they generated and established in their "several quarters"? Lucretius is again explicit:

The first . . . to come together in the midst were all the particles of earth, by reason of their weight and their entanglement, and these all 'gan to take the lowest seats; also the more they came together in communal entanglement, the more they squeezed out such as were to form the sea, sun, moon, and stars, and the walls of the great world. For these are all composed of lighter, rounder seeds than those of earth, and elements much smaller. And so the fiery ether first broke forth, arising from earth's parts through loose-meshed apertures, and, being light, took off much fire with it, . . . for, when all this unites above, then clouds of concrete substance weave their webs aloft beneath the sky. Thus then at that time was the light diffusive ether with its concrete substance poured around and arched on all sides; spreading wide in all directions round about, it thus with greedy grasp enclosed all other things.

Ether was followed by the rudiments of sun and moon, whose globes turn to and fro between it and the earth; which neither earth nor mighty ether has appropriated, since they neither were of weight enough to sink and settle down, nor yet so light that they could glide along the topmost coasts.[13]

He goes on to explain that, after the withdrawal of ether and rudiments of sun and moon from the original chaotic mass, the "earth [i.e., what remains] suddenly sank in, where now the mighty azure tract of sea extends and with a salt flood drenched the hollows."

And day by day, the more the heats of ether round about and the sun's rays compressed the Earth on all sides into narrow limits . . . all the more the salt sweat, squeezed out from her frame, gave increase by its oozing to the sea . . .; the more too did those many particles of heat and air glide forth and fly abroad and far from earth condense the high and gleaming quarters of the sky . . . So then the weighty earth . . . took its place, and all the world's mud, so to speak, flowed heavily into the lowest place and settled at the bottom, like dregs.[14]

This vivid exposition serves well, it seems to me, to amplify Uriel's incomplete account of the World-genesis. Here the sequence-order of generation as well as the hierarchical arrangement of elements and ether is faithfully observed. And both Uriel and Lucretius agree that a part of the purest ether "in circuit walls this Universe."

Other aspects of Uriel's evolving World merit consideration. What, for example, is the relationship between the "ethereal quintessence of Heaven," of which the stars and outmost sphere are made, and the four cumbrous elements? Since the term *quintessence* is used, one might suppose that it refers to the Aristotelean fifth essence, an ethereal substance differing in kind from the four simple bodies.[15] But such an interpretation is not necessarily valid. In fact, it contradicts the tenor of the whole passage; no atomistic philosopher could equate his concept of ether with that of

4/248

Aristotle. The Stoics, moreover, are perhaps the founders of a tradition according to which ether is the result of successive condensations of original fire[16] or the sublimation of the four elements of nature, particularly of air and fire.[17] And one finds this tradition firmly established in the seventeenth century.[18] Comenius, disdaining Aristotle's concept of the fifth element, is especially insistent that natural phenomena are *"all one matter of the world, distinguished by degrees of density and rarity."*[19] There can be only four elements, says he.

That is, there are four faces of the matter of the world reduced into formes . . . differing especially in the degree of rarity and density . . . *The Peripateticks put the sublunary fire, for skie, and call the skie a Quintessence.* But that same sublunary fire is a meer figment; the heaven it selfe, furnished with fiery light, is the highest element of the world . . . He that is not satisfied with these of ours, but seeks more subtile demonstrations, let him see *Campanella, Verulamius,* and *Thomas Lydiat* of the nature of heaven, &c. and he will acknowledge the vanity of the Aristotelicall figment.[20]

What Uriel really intimates is that, just as the alchemist distills a fifth essence out of the four elements, so these same cumbrous elements, especially the lighter fire and air, have been sublimated and refined into purest ether. And this is the "ethereal quintessence" which constitutes the substance of the heavenly bodies and the outmost sphere.[21] Anyone who wishes may conceive a parallel between the Archangel's account of the creation of starry heavens and that recorded as God's work of the fourth day in *Genesis.*

Finally, it must be noted that Uriel seems to be interested only in the ethereal composition of the World's outmost sphere. But since he runs God's errands through all the

Heavens or down to Earth (III, 651), he must also be aware
that this first convex is stationary, firm, and opaque, whose
function is to divide the luminous interior from the inroads
of dark chaos (III, 418 ff.). As messenger he must have
traveled often the way from Heaven through a wide opening
in the World's crust at its zenith down to his present station
in the Sun (III, 526, 529-534). On these matters he is silent,
but he is certainly correct in assuming a traditional outer
shell of the World and that its composition is ethereal. As
Professor McColley says:

. . . the protective outer shell is an expression of a conception
long commonplace in geocentric cosmology. Among the Hebrews it appears as a firmament or a curtain, to the medievalist
Richard of Middleton it is an enclosing surface, and, to retrace,
it is found among the Greeks as a crystal shell, a tunic, a membrane. . . . During the first half of the seventeenth century the
conception is referred to among others by Thomas Tymme, Johannes Johnstonus, and John Swan, with the last saying, 'The
firmament is a vaulted roof . . . as a certain husk, shell, or box,
inclusively containing all things without the Heaven of Heavens.'[22]

Democritus conceives that "the mass of earth, composed
of the atoms which were larger and less mobile, formed the
central point, and the ether, consisting of the smaller and
rounded particles of fire, formed the exterior shell of the
cosmos that was thus composed."[23] Seneca reports an opinion of the atomist Artemidorus with disgust: "Nam, si illi
credimus, summa ora solidissima est, in modum tecti durata
et alti crassique corporis, quod atomi congesti coaceruatique
fecerunt."[24]

Lucretius speaks of the "flaming ramparts of the world"[25]
and, as we have seen, tells how "at that time was the light

diffusive ether with its concrete substance poured around and arched on all sides; spreading wide in all directions round about, it thus with greedy grasp enclosed all other things."[26] Here are shells, curtains, boxes, or membranes enough, but for the most part they are in circular motion, corresponding to the *Primum Mobile* of the Ptolemaic cosmology. Uriel has no use for the *Primum Mobile;* his outmost sphere is firmly and immovably stationary. If he had reported upon this condition, he might have recalled that Epicurus postulates a world-boundary "either rare or dense, either revolving or stationary"[27] with the conclusion that motions of the heavenly bodies "may not impossibly be due to the revolution of the whole heaven, or else it may remain stationary, and they may revolve."[28] At any rate, the creator of Uriel's outmost sphere chooses that it must be dense and stationary[29] while, within, the numberless stars roll orbicular in their appointed courses.

II

Affable Raphael is the divine historian extraordinary, the facile raconteur of remarkable events, mentor of Adam, metaphysician, and indifferent physicist with Stoic or atomistic inclinations. In the course of a single half day, earth time (V, 300, 599—VIII, 630), he expatiates on the nature of God and the metaphysical relationship between man and angels, relates how apostate angels in Heaven were conquered in a three-day battle, Heaven time, and cast into Hell, explains why and in what manner God created the new World including man, and discourses with hesitation on celestial motions in the newly created Cosmos. All of these historical records and reminiscences are of epic importance, but here we are concerned only with his two accounts of World-creation and especially with the order in which phenomena of the material Universe are said to have come into being.

This divine Interpreter's first report on creation of the world lacks something in the way of completeness, order, and clarity. The initial act of Messiah in quieting a portion of chaos and circumscribing in it the form of a globe is dramatic and clear enough: the radiant Son of God appears in his chariot surrounded by a splendid entourage of winged Spirits in winged chariots; the gates of heaven open and let forth the King of Glory, in his powerful Word and Spirit, coming to create new worlds; chaos is discovered to be, as it were, a turbulent sea in wild motion; Messiah stills the waves and orders peace; on the wings of Cherubim and followed by the procession he rides far into chaos, takes the compasses, and circumscribes the Universe, saying, "This be thy just circumference, O world" (VII, 192-231).[30] At this point the Son together with his entourage in celestial equipages—no doubt symbols of God's creative powers and agencies—seem to fade from the scene and are not discovered in procession again until they return after creation to God's house in mid-Heaven (VII, 550-580). But after materials of the Universe have been formed into a sphere, the philosophical Raphael announces abruptly:

Thus God the heaven created, thus the earth,
Matter unformed and void: Darkness profound
Covered the abyss: but on the watery calm
His brooding wings the spirit of God outspread,
And vital virtue infused, and vital warmth
Throughout the fluid mass, but downward purged

The black tartareous cold infernal dregs
Adverse to life: then founded, then conglobed
Like things to like, the rest to several place
Disparted, and between spun out the air,
And earth self balanced on her center hung (VII, 232-242).

In this manner an instantaneous creation is completed[31] with some indication as to the order in which the process is consummated.

When Raphael remarks that God thus created heaven and earth, he means that the portion of chaos thus circumscribed contains heaven and earth *in potentia*. The globe of primitive matter is within itself still formless and covered with profound darkness. And the unorganized mass is said to be in composition "fluid" or further characterized as a "watery calm." Could this mean that, as a second step in creation, the original atomic materials of chaos have been differentiated into "waters"? Here the Archangel, remembering *Genesis*, is involving himself in a pre-*Genesis* tradition which has sometimes been combined with Stoic doctrine concerning the *diacosmesis*. Berosus, formulating Babylonian cosmology, says: "In the beginning all was darkness and water. . . . The All was once fluid; . . . but the god Bel . . . divided the darkness in the midst, and so separated earth and heaven from one another, and therewith established the order of the universe."[32] A speaker in the hermetic *Poimandres* sees a "downward-tending darkness" *(amorphos hyle)* which, says he, "I saw . . . changing into a watery substance, which was unspeakably tossed about,"[33] or more succinctly, "There was darkness in the deep, and water without form."[34] And Stoics assert that the first step in World-genesis is the differentiation of original fire ("through air") into water. This "water" is not water as we know it, but a sort of compound substance

out of which earth and water may later be differentiated.[35]
And Sir Walter Ralegh—quoting Zeno to the effect that
"God turneth the substance of fire by 'air into water'"—continues: "And the word which the Hebrews call *maim* is not
to be understood according to the Latin translation simply,
and as specifical water; but the same more properly signi-
fieth liquor. . . . 'For *maim*,' saith he [Montanus], 'is a dou-
ble liquor'; that is, of diverse natures; 'and this name, or
word, the Latins, wanting a voice to express it, call it in the
plural, *aquas*, waters.'"[36]

Comenius identifies Moses' "waters" and "darkness" with
*"a vapour or a fume . . . a Chaos of dispersed Atomes, co-
hering in no part thereof."*[37] One may reasonably conclude,
it seems to me, that Raphael's "fluid mass" is merely a substance "of diverse natures" and does not represent the differentiation of primitive matter. It is a sort of compound
containing in solution, as it were, all possible elements and
aspects of the visible Universe. In the light of Comenius'
interpretation, it may easily be identified with Uriel's "formless mass" which he sees come to a "heap."

Now comes the second step in the process of creation.
The spirit of God outspreads his brooding wings on the
watery calm and infuses "vital virtue" and "vital warmth"
throughout the fluid mass. I have shown elsewhere that this
"vital virtue" so infused constitutes the forms of all things
invested with life and the capacity of occasional actuation.
Here the Spirit of God communicates to a prepared matter
those creative powers or hidden seeds of things—sometimes
called "seminal reasons" or *logoi spermatikoi*—which are pale
reflections of exemplars in God's mind.[38] Nor does Raphael
forget—as is the case with Uriel—to intimate the source of
renewed motion: the "vital warmth" mentioned is the effect

of an infused but as yet invisible light, one of whose creative powers is to move itself, to heat the mass, and to divide matter into ordered parts.[39] Thus the Spirit which broods upon the waters is not a person but the divine power of God (DC., XV, 13) which impregnates the fluid mass with the seminal forms of all things, with potential life, and, through heating by light, with the possibility of ordered movement. No wonder, then, that Uriel should have discovered his upward-flying ether to be animated or "spirited with various forms, / That rolled orbicular, and turned to stars" (III, 717-718).

Next, under the divine urge of tremendous power-potentials infused into Raphael's fluid mass, cosmic phenomena begin to emerge. The black, tartareous, cold, infernal dregs, adverse to life, are purged downward: in this process, like atoms are conglobed with like[40] in the formation of the four elements; what is left after the downward purging of dregs is "to several place disparted," with the air spun out "between." So far as sequence-order of world-genesis is concerned, this sketch is even more muddled than Uriel's. But perhaps Raphael is trying to synthesize atomistic and hermetic-Stoic cosmology. One hermetic philosopher, attempting to conciliate *Genesis* with Stoic physics, may be able to throw some light on the problem of ordered development:

There was a darkness in the deep, and water without form; and there was a subtle breath [a fine airy substance, or a subtle spirit], intelligent, which permeated the things in Chaos with divine power. Then, when all was yet undistinguished and unwrought, there was shed forth holy light; and the elements came into being. All things were divided one from another, and the lighter things were parted off on high, the fire being suspended aloft, so that it rode upon the air; and the heavier things sank down, and sand was deposited beneath the watery substance,

and the dry land was separated out from the watery substance,
and became solid. And the fiery substance was articulated . . .
and the heaven appeared with its seven spheres . . . visible in
starry forms, with all their constellations.[41]

Here one discovers the familiar waters covered with darkness into which there is infused a subtle spirit—but this time
the *pneuma* of the Stoics.[42] First, light is shed forth, and
under its influence the elements come into being. Then the
lightest element, fire or ether, springs up on high, followed
next by the air; and the heavier elements sink down, being
differentiated into presumably water and solid land. And
the fire or ether is articulated into revolving planets and
stars. Perhaps a similar order is implied in Raphael's sketch:
chaos, impregnation, (infusion of light), conglobing of atoms
into the elements, "the rest [i.e., fire or ether] to several
place disparted," then air spun out between the ethereal
sphere and the earthy, differentiation of the remaining mass
into water and dry land, "And earth, selfbalanced, on her
centre hung"; finally the articulation of ethereal materials
into revolving heavenly bodies. And such implied order of
development is supported in some detail by Raphael's history of creation within six days.

It is clear, however, that the account of creation in a six-
day progression is not complete within itself but must be
supplemented by Raphael's first sketch. Before activities of
the First Day, for example, a chaotic mass of atomic materials[43] has already been calmed, delimited, and impregnated by the Spirit of God. And now on the First Day, a fourth
step is taken: God says, "Let there be Light," and immediately Light, exhaling first from darkness of the mass and
achieving visibility, springs from the Deep in the spherical
form of a radiant cloud, and begins a journey from East to

West through the aery gloom. As a result of this circular motion, light is divided from darkness by the hemisphere, and the World is provided with night and day (VII, 243-356). The ultimate origin and nature of this primitive Light is a profound mystery. Perhaps this is one of the "mighty works" of God to which the Archangel refers when he warns man against vain speculation about matters divinely "suppressed in night" (VII, 111-124). Nevertheless, men have speculated. Some in the seventeenth century particularly have surmised that this Light is fire, or an attenuation of fire, or an efflux from the fiery elements; some say it is a corporeal substance, and in no sense spiritual; others conceive it to have been originally an invisible substance or power permeating all things and finally attaining visibility.[44] One gets the impression that Raphael himself is none too certain as to its nature. He is doubtless philosopher enough, however, to concede that "We cannot form any conception of light independent of a luminary; but we do not therefore infer that a luminary is the same as light, or equal in dignity" (*DC.*, XV, 31). Hence he intimates that Light produced on the First Day may be considered as dual in nature: it is a luminary whose substance—like that of the Sun's body—is ethereal, the pure "quintessence" or ultimate sublimation of air-fire particles capable of receiving the form of a spherical cloud; it is also the active principle of creative energy infused by the Spirit of God into chaos, now exhaled from the permeated mass, concentrated in the ethereal substance, and made visible as radiant light in motion.[45] As luminary substance it may be identified, or at least compared, with the atomist's ether or the hermetic-Stoic "unmixed fire" which leapt forth first from the chaotic mass. But as light or active principle of creative energy it is, on the First Day and on all other Days of creation, the effective and divine power inherent in the fiat, "And God said." And the function of Light so constituted is, as we have seen, to illuminate all things, to move and stimulate the particles of matter in the formation of elements arranged into spheres in accordance with relative density and rarity, and by heating to insure the emergence of embryonic life.[46]

On the First Day, primeval Light makes one complete circuit of the "fluid mass." In this progress it winnows out the lightest particles, conglobes and sublimates elements into an ethereal substance, and thus creates an outer sphere of the Cosmos. This is the "heaven" celebrated by celestial choirs at the Day's end. This is the "clear hyaline, the glassy sea" (VII, 619), the "crystalline sphere" (III, 482), a bright sea of metaphorical jasper or liquid pearl flowing,

> whereon
> Who after came from earth, sailing arrived,
> Wafted by angels, or flew o'er the lake
> Rapt in a chariot drawn by fiery steeds (III, 518-522).

It is the upper "circumfluous waters calm, in wide / Crystalline ocean" on which the World is built. Its function is to protect the interior of the Cosmos from the loud misrule of Chaos, "lest fierce extremes / Contiguous might distemper the whole frame" (VII, 270-273).

Comenius at times seems to identify it with his *"skie . . . the most pure part of the matter of the world, spread over the highest spaces of the world,"* whose nature is to *"be liquid in the highest degree volatile and hot."*[47] He calls it "the first moveable."[48] And in this opinion he is logically correct: for if we consider primitive Light—symbol and executor of God's will—as proximately the First Mover in the process of World-genesis, then that which is "first moved" is certainly the substance of this crystalline sphere spread over the highest spaces of the World. At other times Comenius intimates that the outmost surface-particles of this sea of flowing "waters" become hardened into an ultimate boundary of the whole globe. Says he: "it was necessary, that the matter being scattered by the light rolling about; should flie hither and thither, and coagulate it selfe at the terms of the world on both sides, that in the middle where the light went . . . there should be pure skie; but that on both sides above and below, the mat[ter] hardening it self, should grow thick."[49]

Here one meets again the shell or membrane which, as Uriel says, "walls this Universe." Here it is composed of a "coagulated" and "hardened" film of the upper waters. It also, therefore, may be referred to as "that first moved" (III, 483). Presumably, production of the flowing sea of jasper together with the hardening of its thickened integument constitute a single act of creation on the First Day.

On the Second Day "God said, let there be a firmament / Amid the waters, and let it divide / The waters from the waters." And God's command is obeyed: Light, still dividing night from day by the hemisphere, makes a second journey around that portion of the central mass which remains below the region purified on the First Day's circuit. In the course of this progress, as might be expected, she winnows out, conglobes, and purifies airy-fiery particles, thus creating a region called the firmament,[50] an "expanse of liquid, pure, / Transparent, elemental air." This *expansum* is diffused in extent from what is now left of the "fluid mass"—i.e., an embryonic earth covered with waters—up to the Crystalline ocean of "upper waters," which is, as we have seen, "the uttermost convex of this great round." It thus serves as a "partition firm and sure" dividing "The waters underneath from those above" (VII, 261-273). Or as Raphael cryptically remarks, "and between spun out the air" (VII, 241). This elemental air of the expanse, however, must be considered as varying in degrees of density and rarity: bordering upon the "lower waters" of the earth, it is a comparatively dense atmosphere containing moisture; stretching upward and approaching the belt of "upper waters," it is naturally rarefied and purified into an "ethereal" substance containing fire.[51] Indeed, it is at one time called "the vast ethereal sky" (V, 267).

On the Third Day, circling Light—at God's command—differentiates embryonic earth-materials from surrounding or saturating "waters" and stimulates floral life-germens into actuation. At the moment of original impregnation, it will be remembered, "vital" power and "vital warmth" were infused into the mass so that, as one effect, infernal dregs adverse to life were purged downward. And now the surface of the material globe is satiate with warm and softening moisture which ferments "the great mother to conceive." But first, dry land emerges as familiar mountains, hills, and valleys; the waters are congregated into seas, rivers, and springs. Then every grass, herb, and fruit-tree, "whose seed is in herself," springs forth into active life, spreading a vari-colored investiture over the earth. A dewy mist goes up and waters all the landscape (VII, 276-338). But the firmament above still remains "a liquid, pure, transparent elemental air," no doubt infused with potential forms but devoid of visible bodies.

On the Fourth Day, therefore, the heavenly lights are brought into being. They are established "high" in the ex-

panse or firmament of heaven (VII, 340-344, 349).[52] Uriel
has already explained how the extremely rarefied and attenuated substance in this topmost region of the "elemental
air," which he calls "ethereal quintessence," "Flew upward,
spirited with various forms, / That rolled orbicular, and
turned to stars" (III, 716-717).

Raphael would no doubt agree, except that perhaps he is
not particularly interested in the energic forms of stars. He
does indicate, however, that on the First Day the Sun's body
in potentia was still sojourning within the "cloudy tabernacle" of the impregnated fluid mass (VII, 248). At any
rate, he now proceeds to record the approximate order in
which the celestial phenomena appear: first, the Sun just
rising in the East; then the full Moon setting in the West;
next the other five planets, as illustrated by "the morning
planet," Venus; and finally, the "thousand thousand" fixed
stars, including the Pleiades, "so far remote, with diminution
seen." This arrangement also faithfully reflects the order of
their relative importance in the world. But at first the Sun's
mighty sphere, though composed of ether, is "unlightsome."[53]
Now comes one of the most significant steps in World-
genesis: The greater part of primitive Light is

> Transplanted from her cloudy shrine, and placed
> In the sun's orb, made porous to receive
> And drink the liquid light, firm to retain
> Her gathered beams, great palace now of light
> (VII, 360-363).

That is to say, the active principle of God's creative energy and power—infused by the Word and Spirit into chaos
and made visible on the First Day—is now transferred from
her temporary luminary and poured into a permanent re-

ceptacle, the Sun's body. Henceforth the Sun, by virtue of his Light augmented by minute lights of the fixed stars, is proximate creator of life and other phenomena on the earth (III, 582-586, 609-612). As God's general deputy made visible, he is lord and ruler of the organized Universe.[54] As Raphael concludes: "Now heaven in all her glory shone, and rolled / Her motions, as the great first mover's hand / First wheeled their course" (VII, 499-501).[55]

With the stretching of this magnificent spectacle through the firmament, Raphael closes his record of World-genesis.[56]

In conclusion, it may be noted that the two Archangels are generally in fundamental agreement regarding the processes and order of creation. Their respectively fragmentary accounts, when tentatively amplified, tend to supplement each other so that a definite pattern of the Universe emerges with considerable clarity. Minor discrepancies in reports, if any, may be traced to differences in character and personal viewpoint. Uriel the physicist sketches with enthusiasm what he sees; Raphael records amazing events and, as metaphysician exercising intuitive reason, contemplates profoundly upon their causal relationships. Neither contemns entirely the discursive reasoning of such philosophers as the atomists, hermetists, and Stoics. Both loyal servants of the Omnipotent King are especially impressed by the fact that heaven and earth "declare the glory of God, and the firmament showeth His handiwork." It is therefore fitting that Raphael should represent the Filial Power, deputy Creator of the World, returning in triumphal procession to the great Father, from whom all powers proceed.[57]

Chapter 5

I

THE SUN IN PARADISE LOST IS A COMPLEX GENERATOR
of varied powers by which he controls and regulates
all functions of the Mundane Universe. As ruler crowned
with surpassing glory he looks from his "sole dominion like
the god / Of this new world" (IV, 33). Likewise he has
elsewhere been called "the leader, prince, and ruler of all
the other lights, the soul and principle of order in the world,
of such dimensions that his light illumines and fills the universe."[1] He is the creator and dispenser of life and accordingly may be conceived as "the common father of all mankind."[2] These grandiose generalities may faintly suggest the
Sun's grandeur and power, but they do not indicate the
sources of his energies or precisely how his magnificent
effects are achieved. It is the purpose of this chapter, therefore, to explain if possible his magnetic power over other
planets and stars according to the doctrine of energic forms,
the influence of Light, and to show how he transmutes base
to analyze the altering consistence of the Sun's body under

THE LORDSHIP
OF MILTON'S SUN

matter with which he is constantly fed into ethereal essences
and how these sublimated substances are carried on rays of
Light into combination with earthly humours to produce
wonderful phenomena on Earth.

It is Uriel who furnishes the key to an understanding of
astral forms, their origin, nature, and unique functions. In
a brief sketch of world-genesis, he declaims with awe:

> And this ethereal quintessence of heaven
> Flew upward, spirited with various forms,
> That rolled orbicular, and turned to stars
> Numberless, as thou seest, and how they move;
> Each had his place appointed, each his course (III, 716-720).

But it is Raphael who reveals most clearly the primitive
origin of all forms. In his first account of creation, he observes:

> Thus God the heaven created, thus the earth,
> Matter unformed and void: . . .

but on the watery calm
His brooding wings the spirit of God outspread,
And vital virtue infused . . .
Throughout the fluid mass (VII, 232-237).

I have already shown elsewhere that this "vital virtue" so
infused constitutes the forms of all things invested with life
and the capacity to attain occasional actuation. Here the
Spirit of God communicates to a prepared matter those creative powers or hidden seeds of things—sometimes called
"seminal reasons" or *logoi spermatikoi*—which are pale reflections of exemplars in God's mind.[3] And among these
vital seminal reasons are the energic forms of the Sun, other
planets, and the stars, awaiting *in potentia* for actuation on
the fourth day of creation. Until that day it is said that the
body of the Sun "in a cloudy tabernacle / Sojourned the
while" (VII, 247-248), as yet "unlightsome" (VII, 355). In
the process of creation, even after the separation of elements
and their sublimation into that ethereal quintessence which
flew upward into the clear firmament of heaven,[4] there were
no stars as yet visible. But, as Uriel says, this sublimated
substance was invested with mysterious animating principles; it was "spirited" with various forms which, assimilating
themselves to appetiting quintessence, rolled orbicular and
turned to stars. Here perplexing questions arise. Are these
forms animating the now visible heavenly bodies endowed
with innate energies that determine rotation, adherence to
appointed courses, and maintenance of magnetic positions
in relation to each other? This would seem possible. Can
such forms actually be called quickening and living spirits,
even reasonable and sensitive souls? Many men have thought
so.[5] Perhaps William Gilbert's discussion of the lodestone
and magnetic bodies may throw some light on the nature

of Uriel's forms with which upward-flying quintessence is
said to have been spirited.

Gilbert leaves no doubt regarding the nature and power
of the energic form which enables magnetic bodies, such as
the stars, to attract other magnetic bodies of like nature by
means of innate, primary, and native strength or vigor. "This
form," says he, "is unique and peculiar: it is not what the
Peripatetics call *causa formalis* and *causa specifica in mixtis*
and *secunda forma;* . . . but it is the form of the prime and
principal globes; and it is of the homogeneous and not altered parts thereof, the proper entity and existence which
we may call the primary, radical, and astral form; not Aristotle's prime form, but that unique form which keeps and
orders its own globe. Such form is in each globe—the sun,
the moon, the stars—one; . . . and it is that true magnetic
potency which we call the primary energy. Hence the magnetic nature . . . is implanted in all its real parts according
to a primal and admirable proportion . . . there is in the
earth a magnetic strength or energy (vigor) of its own, as
sun and moon have each its own *forma.*"[6] This innate energy determines the natural verticity or rotation of celestial
globes, their circular motions, and an admirable concord in
their respectively emanated magnetic influence. In the heavens, therefore, "no violence is offered to bodies, there are
no strifes or discords; but here we have, as the condition of
the world holding together, a concerted action,—to wit, an
accordance of the perfect, homogeneous parts of the world's
globes with the whole, a mutual agreement of the chief
forces therein for soundness, continuity, position, direction,
and unity."[7]

This concord in the heavens is achieved by virtue of the
fact that in each case the unique rays of magnetic force are

dispersed in all directions, i.e., spherically, around the body. "And as light . . . arrives instantly . . . with far greater instantaneousness, the magnetic energy is present within the limits of its forces; and because its act is far more subtile than light, and it does not accord with non-magnetic bodies, it has no relations with air, water, or other non-magnetic body; neither does it act on magnetic bodies by means of forces that rush upon them with any motion whatever, but being present solicits bodies that are in amicable relations to it self."[8] Thus the mutual forces inherent in magnetic spheres surrounding heavenly bodies cause "that rush toward union which commonly is called attraction."[9] But the center of this attracting magnetic sphere is not in the pole: each body's center is the center of that body's magnetic movements.[10] While each celestial globe moves of itself or is moved naturally by its primary form, it must necessarily be incited or propelled in some measure by magnetic energies emanating from other planets and stars.[11] And the controlling power in this complex interplay of magnetic forces in the universe is the sun. As Gilbert concludes: "Thus, inasmuch as the sun itself is the mover and inciter of the universe, the other planets that are situate within the sphere of his forces, being impelled and set in motion, do also with their own forces determine their own courses and revolve in their own periods, according to the amplitude of their greater rotation and the differences of the forces effused."[12]

Other thinkers of the seventeenth century are aware of the controversy over the nature of energic forms. Hakewill, for example, observes of the heavenly bodies that they "haue a *forme* giuen them, which differeth from the *formes* of all corruptible Bodies, so far as it suffereth not, nor can it suffer from any of them, being so excellent and perfect in it selfe,

as it wholly satiateth the appetite of the *matter* it inform-
eth."[13] And Robert Boyle asserts that "those eminent stars
and planets . . . are not to be considered by us as sluggish
inergetical bodies, or as if they were set only to be as bare
candles to us, but as bodies full of proper motion, or peculiar operation, and of life; the sun not only shining upon
the rest of the planets, but, by his quickening warmth,
awakening, stirring, and raising, the motions, properties, and
powers, that are peculiar to them."[14] He is further of the
opinion that "our planet . . . is not only enlightened . . . by
the power, virtue, and influence of the sun, but hath its
proper magnetical planetary virtue also fermented, stirred,
agitated and awakened in it, which it remits back with the
reflected light of the sun."[15] In the light of such opinions,
it would seem reasonable to suppose that Uriel's forms animating upward-flying quintessence are none other than those
unique forms, sources of magnetic energies, postulated and
defended by Gilbert, Hakewill, Boyle, and others in the
seventeenth century. But whether the angel's phrase "spirited with various forms" can be interpreted to mean animated by living, reasonable, and sensitive souls is a question
subject to controversy.

Gilbert, marveling at the wonderful magnetic powers effused from celestial bodies, agrees enthusiastically with the
ancients that there must exist a living soul in each of the
stars, in the sun, moon, and other planets. "As for us," he
exclaims, "we find this soul only in the globes and in their
homogeneous parts, and albeit this soul is not in all the
globes the same (for that in the sun or in certain stars is
much superior to that in other less noble globes). Still in
very many globes the souls agree in their powers. Thus,
each homogenic part tends to its own globe and inclines in

the direction common to the whole world, and in all globes
the effused forms reach out and are projected in a sphere all
round, and have their own bounds—hence the order and
regularity of all the motions and revolutions of the planets
. . . wherefore Aristotle concedes to the spheres and heavenly orbs (which he imagines) a soul, for the reason that
they are capable of circular motion and action and that they
move in fixed, definite tracks. . . . As for us, we deem the
whole world animate, and all globes, all stars, and this
glorious earth, too, we hold to be from the beginning by
their own destinate souls governed and from them also to
have the impulse of self-preservation."[16] Such astral souls
do not possess visible organs; their operations are other than
those discovered in nature and in animals.[17] They are without senses, but as living entities the globes "endure, rotate,
and move in orbits, and without wasting or weariness run
their courses."[18] Hakewill, on the contrary, will have nothing to do with astral souls. He agrees with Espence that
"what is denied those Bodies in *life,* in *sense,* in *reason,* is
abundantly supplied in their constant and unchangeable
duration, arising from that inviolable knot, and indissoluble
marriage, betwixt the *matter* & the *forme.*"[19] Now though
Uriel as spirit is indeed Regent of the Sun, one may doubt
whether any of the heavenly bodies in his newly created
world are endowed with souls. Raphael, to be sure, surmises
that every star is "perhaps a world / Of destined habitation"
(VII, 621-622) and imagines that other Suns, with attendant
Moons, may be discovered "Communicating male and female light, / Which two great sexes animate the world, /
Stored in each orb perhaps with some that live" (VIII, 150-
152). And Satan, flying past innumerable stars on his way
to the Sun, notes that some of them seem happy isles like

the Hesperian Gardens of old (III, 567-568). But the presence of life-forms on a planet does not necessarily imply the existence there of a world-soul.

There can be no doubt, however, that the author of *Paradise Lost* espouses the doctrine of energic forms in his representation of the Sun as magnetic center and ruler of a magnetized world. Of the great luminary in relation to other celestial bodies, it is recorded:

> they as they move
> Their starry dance in numbers that compute
> Days, months, and years, towards his all-cheering lamp
> Turn swift their various motions, or are turned
> By his magnetic beam, that gently warms
> The universe, and to each inward part
> With gentle penetration, though unseen,
> Shoots invisible virtue even to the deep:
> So wondrously was set his station (III, 579-587).

And Raphael, questioning the possibility of a heliocentric universe, asks:

> What if the sun
> Be center to the world, and other stars
> By his attractive virtue and their own
> Incited, dance about him various rounds? (VIII, 122-125).

Analysis of these passages reveals what seems to be an evident accord with the magnetic principles supported by Gilbert and others. Here the stars, incited by their individual energic forms or unique magnetic potencies, turn swift their various motions and are also propelled by the Sun's magnetic beams. By reason of their own attractive virtue acting in concord with that of the Sun, they perhaps dance about him various rounds. Or as Gilbert says: "Inasmuch as the sun itself is the mover and inciter of the universe, the other planets that are situate within the sphere of his forces, being impelled and set in motion, do also with their own forces determine their own courses and revolve in their own periods." Moreover, the Sun's magnetic energies are invisible and act upon each inward part of other magnetic bodies with gentle penetration. Or as Gilbert has it: The magnetic nature of a body "is implanted in all its real parts according to a primal and admirable proportion," and effused energy does not act on the unified parts of magnetic bodies "by means of forces that rush upon them with any motion whatever, but being present solicits bodies that are in amicable relations to it self." And finally, the Sun is said to shoot "invisible virtue even to the deep." This means, one may suppose, that the Sun's magnetic beam, more subtle than light, penetrates even to the center of other magnetic bodies, for, as Gilbert observes, "The earth's centre is the centre of the earth's magnetic movements."[20]

So much may be said of Uriel's energic forms and of the magnetic powers effused from celestial bodies, energies unique and interacting in concord. But whether the world's physical structure be considered heliocentric or geocentric, the magnetic center and ruler of the universe is the lordly Sun. Here may be discovered one, perhaps the principal, source of his tremendous power.

II

Uriel will have it that the substance of all celestial bodies is "ethereal quintessence," and Raphael affirms that the Sun's mighty sphere is "of ethereal mold" (VII, 356). I have shown elsewhere that this ethereal quintessence is atomic in consistence, being an attenuated sublimation of the four elements or particularly of air and fire.[21] But the significant consideration for us here is that the bodies of celestial globes are subject to *metabole* or internal change though not to dissolution. "For the permanence of every kind of body," says the hermetic philosopher, "is maintained by change. Immortal bodies undergo change without dissolution, but the changes of mortal bodies are accompanied by dissolution; that is the difference between immortals and mortals."[22] Raphael is acquainted with this doctrine: "For know," says he, "whatever was created needs / To be sustained and fed" (V, 414-415). He goes on to explain just how this process of feeding the celestial spheres takes place:

> of elements
> The grosser feeds the purer, earth the sea,
> Earth and sea feed air, the air those fires
> Ethereal, and as lowest first the moon;
> Whence in her visage round those spots, unpurged
> Vapours not yet into her substance turned.
> Nor doth the moon no nourishment exhale
> From her moist continent to higher orbs.
> The sun that light imparts to all, receives
> From all his alimental recompense
> In humid exhalations, and at even
> Sups with the ocean (V, 413-426).

This exposition is evidently based in part upon Stoic philosophy regarding the cyclic transmutation of the four elements and their upward and downward movement. Lucilius Balbus, Cicero's defender of Stoicism, explains how in nature "earth turns to water, water into air, and air into aether [or fire], and then the process is reversed, and aether becomes air, air water, and water earth. . . . Thus the parts of the

world are held in union by the constant passing up and
down . . . of these four elements."[23] Since the stars are of
a fiery nature, "they are nourished by the vapors of the
earth, the sea and the waters, which are raised up by the
sun out of the field which it warms and out of the waters;
and when nourished and renewed by these vapors the stars
. . . shed them back again."[24] Cleanthes is of the opinion,
therefore, that the sun itself, being made of aether or fire,[25]
"is nourished by the vapors exhaled from the ocean because
no fire could continue to exist without sustenance of some
sort."[26] And Chrysippus agrees that "the stars are, with the
sun, kindled from the sea."[27] It would seem, then, that
Raphael is correct when in strict Stoic terms he conceives
of an alimentary process taking place in the bodies of sun
and stars. He intimates that by some sort of concoction certain crude materials are turned into the Moon's substance,
though her spots may represent undigested vapors exhaled
from her moist continent to higher orbs. But for him all the
stars are ethereal "fires," and like them the Sun receives his
alimental recompense in humid exhalations, and at even
sups with the ocean.

Satan in his flight through the cosmos discovers the Sun's
ethereal body, fed by exhalations from earth, to be informed
by radiant light and consequently undergoing constantly a
mysterious process of *metabole* or transmutation of humid
materials into its own substance (III, 593-608). Aside from
the awe-inspiring brilliance of light everywhere, he seems
somewhat perplexed to find that not all parts of the solar
landscape are alike and is uncertain as to whether the various parts might be considered metal or stone. If metal, part
seems to him gold, part clear silver; if stone, largely carbuncle or chrysolite, ruby or topaz, or perhaps the twelve

that shone on Aaron's breastplate. Here appears suggestive evidence that not all exhalations received by the Sun from earth have been completely assimilated or digested, as it were, into the same degree of purity or perfection. The stones mentioned are not intended, to be sure, to indicate any particular state or development of solar substance— though solar atoms do participate, of course, in the creation of earthly gems; here their names are introduced mainly to suggest, because of their traditional innate brightness,[28] the extreme radiance of certain parts of the Sun's composition. But the primitive metals, gold and silver—glowing with light as iron with fire—must be linked with alchemical transmutations churning in the Sun's body. The result of such activities is the attainment there of that stone which philosophers on earth have so long sought in vain. Satan is permitted to witness the ultimate state of the Sun's *metabole,* the perfected magisterium: "What wonder then if fields and regions here / Breathe forth elixir pure, and rivers run / Potable gold" (III, 606-608).

But the alchemical processes here suggested are complicated and extremely mystifying. If Satan is an exoteric, he will identify the metals he sees with actual gold and silver; if he is an esoteric impressed by the implied colors, red and white, he will identify what "seemed" to be gold and clear silver with the famous alchemical *Sol* and *Luna,* respectively "sophic sulphur" and "sophic mercury."[29] In either case most alchemists agree that *Sol* and *Luna,* gold and silver, are the ultimate or primary materials of the philosopher's stone. Arnald of Villanova, for example, quotes Avicenna to the effect that "unless I should see gold and silver, I should certainly say that alchemy is not a true art."[30] Arnald himself, discussing the red and white tincts of the elixir's material, concludes, "Its father is *Sol; Luna* is its mother, for from these bodies . . . is our medicine extracted."[31] And Paracelsus is explicit: "This is what Hermes asserts in the following terms: 'The Sun and the Moon are the roots of this Art.' The Son of Hamuel says that the Stone of the philosophers is water coagulated, namely, in Sol and Luna. From this it is clearer than the sun that the material of the Stone is nothing else but Sol and Luna. . . . We know that there are only two Stones, the white and the red. There are also two matters of the Stone, Sol and Luna."[32] Now "sophic mercury" (Luna) and "sophic sulphur" (Sol) must be carefully distinguished from common mercury and sulphur. John Read observes: "The view was widely held among mediaeval alchemists that when ordinary mercury (or silver) and gold were divested of their grosser (physical) properties, they yielded 'philosophical' or 'sophic' mercury and sulphur. . . . Sophic mercury was often called 'fixed' mercury, that is, the solid essence or core of mercury."[33] Paracelsus agrees: "With regard to the generation of Gold, the true opinion is that it is Sulphur sublimated to the highest degree . . . and purged from all dregs, blackness, and filth whatever. . . . Sulphur . . . is the first matter of gold. . . . This is the Sulphur of the Philosophers, from which gold is produced, not that other Sulphur from which come iron, copper, etc."[34] We may safely conclude, it seems to me, that Satan is probably an esoteric: what "seemed" to him gold on the Sun is none other than the alchemical Sol, that is, "sophic sulphur," "sulphur of the philosophers," the ultimately cleansed and sublimated essence of sulphur; what seemed "silver clear" is Luna, "sophic" or "fixed" mercury, the solid and essential core of mercury. From the marriage of these two—the red and white tinctures—is born that pure elixir which breathes

forth from the solar fields and regions. One acquainted with
the symbolic language of the alchemists may advisedly speak
concerning the "marriage" of these two. For in esoteric
literature, John Read notes, "The King and Queen, or Sol
and Luna, were alchemical designations for the masculine
and feminine principles respectively."[35] Paracelsus explains
why, in producing the magistery, it is necessary to have "Sol
and Luna, formed together in proper marriage:" "As we
see that the man or the woman, without the seed of both,
cannot generate, in the same way our man, Sol, and his wife,
Luna, cannot conceive, or do anything in the way of generation, without the seed and sperm of both. Hence the
philosophers gathered that a third thing is necessary, namely, the animated seed of both, the man and the woman,
without which they judged that the whole of their work
was fruitless and in vain."[36] And Thomas Norton, skilled in
the use of obscure language, closes his advice to the adepts
with a quotation from Hermes:

> *Candida tunc rubeo jacet uxor nupta marito,*
> That is to saie, if ye take heede therto,
> Then is the faire White Woman
> Married to the Ruddy Man . . .
> For then compleate is made our *Stone.*[37]

It need cause no surprise to discover the male and female
principles operating harmoniously together in the Sun when
one recalls Raphael's dictum, "Which two great sexes animate the world."

Milton the poet may be praised for not attempting to
reduce to poetic terms the processes involved in the production of elixir from Sol and Luna. But with tongue in cheek
and with his usual flair for symbolic references to classical

mythology, he does credit earthly alchemists with having found sophic sulphur and sophic mercury. Philosophers here below have sought the imagined Stone in vain, he says,

> In vain, though by their powerful art they bind
> Volatile Hermes, and call up unbound
> In various shapes old Proteus from the sea,
> Drained through a limbec to his native form (III, 602-605).

This "Hermes" is without doubt mercury or quicksilver (argent vive), one of the most volatile of metals. Before alchemists can employ it as one of the "seeds" of the elixir, they must reduce it to a so-called "fixed" state. Now Geber defines fixation as the "convenient disposing a *Fugitive* Thing, to abide and sustain the *Fire*. The *Cause* of the *Invention* of this *Fixation*, is, that every *Tincture*, and every *Alteration*, may be perpetuated in the Thing altered, and not changed."[38] The ultimate purification of mercury, he says, may best be accomplished by reiterated sublimation. And the sublimation of argent vive "is compleated, when its *Terrestreity* is highly purified, and its *Aquosity* wholly removed."[39] With the removal of earth, water, and other impurities, the inner core or essence of mercury remains hard and stable. This is the result when philosophers "bind volatile Hermes." This is, as we have seen, what alchemists often call "sophic mercury." But that metal, symbolized by the myth of shape-shifting Proteus,[40] is not so easily identified. Alchemists are said to call it up—as Proteus was called from the sea—"unbound / In various shapes" and finally to drain it through a limbec to its "native form." This is a cryptic saying. But sulphur and the situation would seem to satisfy all requirements. In alchemical processes sulphur certainly assumes a great variety of forms and colors; it too can be reduced to a "fixed" state. In its original form, Geber says, "*Sulphur* is a fatness of the *Earth,* by temperate *Decoction* in the *Mine* of *Earth* thickened, until it is hardened and made dry."[41] When mixed with other metals, it not only changes form but also assumes a variety of colors: violet, or red, or "a *Celestial* and *Delightful Colour;*"[42] there is a "red and white Sulphur of Marcasites, a yellow, red, and black Sulphur of Talc, a purple and black Sulphur of Cachimiae."[43] Paracelsus records three kinds or states of sulphur: (a) "resin of the earth . . . mother and father of all others," (b) "embryonated," where it passes from the hard to the volatile stage, and (c) "animated" or "Spagyric," which is repurged from the other two and "exists Spagyrically pure from all superfluities."[44] He goes on to say that purification may be attained by sublimation or descension, though sometimes the use of aquafortis and coagulation are necessary.[45] But for the "fixing" of sulphur, Geber relies mainly on reiterated and rapid sublimation in the aludel or in a sublimatory furnace resembling the alembic.[46] One may reasonably conclude, then, that this "Proteus" is none other than sulphur, at first "unbound" and consequently changing form, shape, color in combination with other metals, and finally in the process of being "drained through a limbec" by repeated sublimation becoming completely purified into "Spagyric" sulphur, i.e., the ultimate core and essence of sulphur. This, I take it, is his "native form"; this is "sophic sulphur," the necessary masculine "seed" in the production of the magistery. Now when philosophers here below can perform such marvels, what wonder then if on the Sun, where Sol and Luna seem plentiful, pure elixir should breathe forth from plain and region.

Since on the Sun elixir does breathe forth, one might ex-

pect that, as an effect of its transmuting action, "rivers run
Potable gold." Paracelsus philosophizes that "Of all elixirs,
the highest and most potent is gold";[47] the Stone of the
Philosophers is a species of Elementary Gold, "as being the
most pure portion of all metallic elements after its purification, when it is termed living philosophical gold. A perfect
equilibrium and equality of the four elements . . . will be-
get the lawful Son of the Sun."[48] He goes on to explain that
wherever this elixir of gold "is brought to bear on anything,
it so transmutes it that it remains . . . in a form similar to
itself."[49] Thus by an alchemical process called "projection"
any matter touched by the elixir (or "stone," or "medicine,"
or "magistery") is transmuted into "potable gold."[50] Roger
Bacon defines alchemy as "a Science teaching how to make
and compound a certaine medicine, which is called *Elixir*,
the which when it is cast upon metalls or imperfect bodies,
doth fully perfect them in the verie projection."[51] This perfected substance, potable or drinkable gold, is sometimes
called Astral Gold, says Paracelsus, having "its centre in the
sun, which communicates it by its rays to all inferior beings.
It is an igneous substance, which receives a continual emanation of solar corpustles that penetrate all things sentient,
vegetable, and mineral."[52] It is supposed to have something
to do with life and the maintenance of health and lon-
gevity.[53]

But in the meantime nothing lives on the Sun except Uriel
and his visitor, Satan. Here is an exceedingly effulgent landscape where all is sunshine without shade; nowhere else can
"air" be found so clear. But to the human eye there seems
little accustomed beauty anywhere. Here immeasurable
forces are at work transmuting constantly inflowing exhalations from earth into Sol and Luna, into elixir and rivers of

potable gold. The luminary is a gorgeous atomic pile, as it were, generating as yet unharnessed and sterile energies. The great Palace of Light shoots forth its beams—but to what purpose? No wonder, then, that Raphael should speak of "the sun that barren shines, / Whose virtue on itself works no effect" (VIII, 94-95).[54] Still, the *metabole* taking place in the solar body, the transformation of crude or refined materials into transportable and useful forms, constitutes a second main source of the Sun's overwhelming power in the universe.

III

This splendid generator of powers, the Sun, must be considered always as a dual entity. He is, as we have seen, a luminary (*lumen*) of ethereal or material mold undergoing alimentary processes; he is also that Light (*lux*) which, on the fourth day of creation, was poured "In the sun's orb, made porous to receive / And drink the liquid light, firm to retain / Her gathered beams" (VII, 359-362).[55] But the precise nature of Miltonic Light—and its consistence, if any[56]— remains somewhat of a mystery. I have identified it elsewhere with "the active principle of creative energy infused by the Spirit of God into chaos, now exhaled from the permeated mass, concentrated in the ethereal substance, and made visible as radiant light in motion."[57] As active principle of creative energy it is, on the First Day and on all other Days of creation, the effective and divine power inherent in the fiat, "And God said." Though most of this creative energy is placed in the Sun's orb, portions of it are in other celestial bodies and in the *rationes seminales* awaiting quickening into actuation. And after the Six Days of creation under the immediate influence of Light, the Son of God, deputy Creator, returns in company with his entourage of celestial equipages to God's house in mid-Heaven (VII, 550-580). Thus the Sun, *lumen* and *lux,* is left as the proximate god of this new World to rule alone, control, and regulate all functions of the Mundane Universe.

But Milton himself seems at times deeply perplexed over the ultimate origin of that mysterious *lux* or light which flows from the Sun. Having escaped the Stygian Pool, he exclaims:

> Hail, holy light, offspring of heaven first-born,
> Or of the eternal coeternal beam
> May I express thee unblamed? Since God is light
> And never but in unapproached light
> Dwelt from eternity, dwelt then in thee,
> Bright effluence of bright essence increate.
> Or hearest thou rather pure ethereal stream
> Whose fountain who shall tell? (III, 1-8).

Here he surmises that sunlight may be identified without blame as a beam coeternal with the Eternal: since God, the metaphysical Abstraction,[58] is said to be Light and to have dwelt from eternity in unapproached light, then this light of the Sun is none other than a portion of the mantle of God, that light which is the bright effluence of his bright, uncreated essence. Or if one may consider God in the mode of his operational existence,[59] i.e., as direct or indirect creator of all things, then holy Light is the first-born offspring of heaven or perhaps the offspring of first-born heaven. In either case Light is to be identified symbolically with God's emanating power and energy as employed by a hierarchy of causes in the creation of the universe. But whether in the emanative process this Light is the first-born offspring of heaven or the offspring of first-born heaven is not clear. At any rate, when Milton in the *De Doctrina Christiana* considers the creation of things invisible and visible, he finds that "The first place is due to things invisible, if not in respect of origin, at least of dignity. For the highest heaven is as it were the supreme citadel and habitation of God." This is the "heaven of heavens," "far above all heavens," where God "dwelleth in the light which no man can approach unto." And, he concludes, "Out of this light it appears that pleasures and glories, and a kind of perpetual heaven, have emanated and subsist" (XV, 29). Here it would seem that the Heaven of Heavens is emanated from that light which surrounds God and that it may be considered the first-born, invisible creation, "if not in respect of origin, at least of dignity." Its origin is probably much more ancient than that of the visible World, and consequently the highest heaven must be carefully distinguished from that heaven which is visible to us; it was of the latter "that Moses undertook to write" (XV, 31).

In the meantime, long before creation of the visible World was perhaps contemplated, this habitation of the "ethereal king" (II, 978) was blazing with creative Light perpetually. On its relation to the Almighty, a multitude of elect Spirits, with locks enwreathed with beams, sing:

> Thee father first they sung omnipotent,
> Immutable, immortal, infinite,
> Eternal king; thee author of all being,
> Fountain of light, thyself invisible
> Amidst the glorious brightness where thou sittest
> Throned inaccessible, but when thou shadest
> The full blaze of thy beams, and through a cloud

Drawn round about thee like a radiant shrine,
Dark with excessive bright thy skirts appear,
Yet dazzle heaven (III, 373-381).

This is that "pure ethereal stream," that heavenly Light, which is the manifestation and symbol of the Ethereal King's power, energy, and glory. But because the mysterious being of God himself is eternally hidden, even though the angels may say, "He is the fountain of Light," what heart of man can comprehend or what words or tongue of Seraph can suffice (VII, 113-114) to "tell" or describe this Fountain except by enumeration of his attributes? This is that "heaven's ray" which creates, tempers, and sustains the landscape of Heaven's ethereous continent (VI, 473-481). And on the countenance of God's Son is impressed the effulgence of the Father's glory and might. So that as the Divine Similitude goes forth to create the visible World, he is crowned with radiance of divine majesty and girt with omnipotent power (VII, 195-196). He transmits a portion of this celestial Light or creative energy from Heaven into a defined part of chaos where it becomes instrumental in the creation of the visible cosmos. This is that "holy light," now clearly recognized as the "offspring" of the first-born invisible heaven of heavens, which invested as with a mantle the rising world of waters "Won from the void and formless infinite" (III, 10-12). It is this same light which, as invisible energy permeating the chaotic mass, exhaled from darkness and became visible when God said, "Let there be light." And it is the same creative light which, on the fourth day of creation, was poured into the Sun's body and which is now apotheosized by the epic poet.[60]

Having escaped Milton's ontological speculations about

light, we may now return to His Lordship, the Sun, question how sunlight is transmitted through the ether, how it sustains other stars, and how its effects are produced upon the earth. The poet does not seem to be greatly interested if at all in the physics of light-transmission. He does espouse, as we have seen, the Stoic philosophy regarding transmutation of the four elements and their upward movement, but he ignores the corresponding downward movement as represented by that philosophy. The Sun's liquid light, however, must illuminate and in certain cases warm the mundane universe. And in some way those earthly and lunar exhalations which are sublimated in the Sun's body must also be shed down as vital recompense to the earth. One might perhaps suppose that, since the material cosmos of *Paradise Lost* is essentially atomic in structure, Milton would have seized upon the Cartesian hypothesis concerning the propagation of light through a fluid medium. As Professor E. T. Whittaker says:

According to the Cartesian philosophy, all space—even at the remotest distances beyond the stars—is a plenum, so that a particle can move only by taking the place of other particles which are themselves displaced. Light was imagined to be essentially a pressure transmitted through this dense mass of particles; vision might therefore be compared to the perception of the presence of objects which a blind man obtains by the use of his stick, the transmission of pressure along the stick from the object to the hand being analogous to the transmission from a luminous object to the eye.[61]

Others have explained the Cartesian "pression" or pressure to "mean a kind of motion which is impressed and propagated through a Fluid Medium."[62] In 1672 Sir Isaac Newton speaks disparagingly of certain "Mechanical Hypotheses on which Light is supposed to be caused by any Pression or Motion whatever, excited in the aether by the agitated parts of Luminous bodies."[63] But that Milton was acquainted with this popular seventeenth-century theory is not certain. It may be significant, however, that in the description of the gorgeously colored landscape of Eden occurs this observation:

> Blossoms and fruits at once of golden hue
> Appeared, with gay enamelled colours mixed:
> On which the sun more glad impressed his beams
> Than in fair evening cloud, or humid bow,
> When God hath showered the earth (IV, 148-152).

And of God's Son it is said: "on thee / Impressed the effulgence of his glory abides, / Transfused on thee his ample spirit rests" (III, 387-389). It would seem that this term *impressed,* thus associated with the effects of light, may possibly be considered as equivalent in meaning to the Cartesian concept of *pression.* But in the absence of further evidence, I would not place too much pressure upon acceptance of the identification.

Be that as it may, the Sun aided by the stars illuminates the cosmos and emanates a holy light (*lux*) "that gently warms / The universe" (III, 583-584) and as life-producing energy heats "Earth's inmost womb" (V, 300-301). Satan complains that in general the terrestrial heaven is filled with "officious lamps" (including the Sun) that shine for Adam alone, in him "concentrating all their precious beams / Of sacred influence." He concludes:

>   in thee
> Not in themselves, all their known virtue appears
> Productive in herb, plant, and nobler birth

Of creatures animate with gradual life
Of growth, sense, reason, all summed up in man
(IX, 103-113).

Dear, accomplished Eve wishes to know why these stars shine all night long, and her disposer Adam replies:

Ministering light prepared, they set and rise;
Lest total darkness should by night regain
Her old possession, and extinguish life
In nature and all things, which these soft fires
Not only enlighten, but with kindly heat
Of various influence foment and warm,
Temper or nourish, or in part shed down
Their stellar virtue on all kinds that grow
On earth, made hereby apter to receive
Perfection from the sun's more potent ray (IV, 664-673).

These stars and planets draw light from the Sun, augmenting by "tincture or reflection" their own "small peculiar" (VII, 364-368). And in contemplation of the solar landscape which breathes forth light-produced power in the form of pure elixir, why should one wonder, says Milton,

when with one virtuous touch
The arch-chemic sun so far from us remote
Produces with terrestrial humor mixed
Here in the dark so many precious things
Of color glorious and effect so rare? (III, 606-612).

Here in these passages is to be found a sufficiency of poetic phrasing, but the physics involved is generally hazy, and except by implication indeterminate. The Sun by day and the stars by night send down upon the earth creative light or stellar "virtue" which foments, warms, tempers, and nourishes all kinds that grow, including all vegetable and animate phenomena; the arch-chemic Sun, mixing light with terrestrial humors, "produces" here in the dark many precious things, colored and rare. But we are left in the dark regarding the precise processes by which these wonders are produced.

But Milton is not more vague in these matters than most of his contemporaries. Hakewill, for example, observes: "The *light* of *Heaven* . . . is not more *comfortable* and *vseful,* than the warmth thereof. . . . Some there are that liue without the *light* of heaven . . . but none without the *warmth,* it being in a manner the *vniversall instrument* of *Nature.*"[64] Boyle will have it that our planet, the earth, is "enlightened, warmed, cherished, and fructified by the power, virtue and influence of the sun; . . . and together with the magnetic planetary property of the earth, which is stirred and raised by the sun, are awakened also the seminal dispositions, odours and ferments, that are lodged in, and proper unto particular regions or places."[65] But recently Professor W. B. Hunter has elucidated admirably certain Miltonic implications regarding the function of *Lux* by reference to Hermetic philosophy. He shows that, for the Hermetist as for Milton, the Sun by means of the light which he emits is the creator and sustainer of all life in the mundane universe.[66] As the Hermetist says: "He assigns to the immortals [i.e., the heavenly bodies] their everlasting permanence . . . ; but with the light which is shed downward, and illuminates all the sphere of water, earth, and air, he puts life into the things in this region . . . and stirs them up to birth, and by successive changes remakes the living creatures and transforms them. . . . And as the light of the sun is poured forth continuously, so his production of life also is continuous and without intermission."[67] Perpetually the emitted light of the Sun, after circulating through the universe upon its life-producing journey, returns to its palace, the Sun's body. One may question, however, Hunter's identification of sunlight with life itself; the creative energy placed in the Sun does not, as he suggests, become "the source for replenishment of the life principle throughout the universe."[68] Life is not generated in the Sun, nor does it return there when a living body suffers dissolution. Light of the Sun is creative only in the sense that it foments, awakens, nourishes, and sustains those seminal virtues, including all life-forms, with which the Spirit of God impregnated the defined fluid mass at creation.[69]

Milton indicates one other complex function of the Sun's virtuous touch. He tells us that rays of the arch-chemic Sun, when mixed with terrestrial humor in the dark, produce many precious things of glorious color and rare effect.[70] In an excellent study, "The Natural History of Metals and Minerals in the Universe of Milton's *Paradise Lost*," Professor E. H. Duncan concludes: "Surely those things of such glorious color and such rare effect produced . . . in the earth, include metals and gleaming mineral gems . . . ; its metaphors express a profound truth for the universe of *Paradise Lost*: that the sun is the repository of occult virtues which are shed thence upon 'all kinds that grow.' "[71] But he does not interpret precisely the nature of those solar virtues or just how they produce rare effects by mixture with terrestrial humour. Any adequate explanation of this additional power of the Sun to produce metals and gems in the earth must take into account the alchemical processes taking place in the solar body. We have already demonstrated how ma-

terials exhaled from the earth feed the Sun's ethereal body
and how they are transmuted by Light into quintessential
elixir, so that rivers there run with potable gold. This entire process is useless unless these materials, sublimated into
the true magistery, can be projected back upon the seminal
virtues of metals and gems locked up in the bowels of the
earth. And this process of projection is accomplished by
the Sun's beams laden with the infinitely sublimated atoms
of potable gold. Paracelsus identifies potable gold, as we
have seen, with Astral Gold, having "its centre in the sun,
which communicates it by its rays to all inferior beings. It
is an igneous substance, which receives a continual emanation of solar corpustles that penetrate all things sentient,
vegetable, and mineral."

But just how that alchemist, the Sun—aided by his yeo-
men, the stars—causes metals and gems to grow in the earth
requires further consideration. Milton himself furnishes by
implication a possible key to the solution of the problem:
he says that the stars *temper* all kinds that grow and that
the Sun's rays mix with terrestrial *humor*. Now these terms,
humor and temper, have alchemical or chemical significance
when applied to processes and elements of metal-production.
Aristotle finds that one variety of earthly bodies is caused
by what he calls "vapourous exhalation." Says he: "The
vapourous exhalation is the cause of all metals, those bodies
which are either fusible or malleable such as iron, copper,
gold. All these originate from the imprisonment of vapourous exhalation in the earth and especially in stones."[72] Perhaps one might safely equate Milton's terrestrial *humor* with
Aristotle's *vapourous exhalation.* The latter's second variety
of exhalation, the "smoky" or "dry"—which he says causes

"the kinds of stones that cannot be melted"[73]—also becomes involved when the Arabians postulate the sulphur-mercury hypothesis of how metals originate. Geber, for example, is reported to have modified the Aristotelian theory as follows: "The two exhalations, he believed, when imprisoned in the bowels of the earth, were not immediately changed into minerals and metals, but underwent an intermediate conversion. The dry or smoky exhalation was converted into sulphur and the watery one into mercury, and it was only by subsequent combination of sulphur and mercury that metals were formed."[74] This sulphur-mercury hypothesis seems to have been generally though not unanimously accepted in the seventeenth century.[75] In his discussion of minerals and metals John Webster observes: "They are said to grow of sulphur and argent vive mixt and tempered together."[76] He goes on to explain: "to make a perfect mixt body, the four Elements do concur: and to make the mixture more perfect, these must be resolved into vapour or exhalation, by the heat of fire, or influence from the Sun and other Planets, as the efficient cause of their generation."[77] Accordingly, Du Bartas praises the Sun's heat,

> which subtilly doth pearce
> The solid thickness of the Vniverse,
> Which in th' Earths kidnyes *Mercury* doth burn,
> And pallid *Sulphur* to bright Metall turn.[78]

And in explanation of why various sorts of metals are produced, Holmyard summarizes Geber: "The reason of the existence of different varieties of metals is that the sulphur and mercury are not always pure and that they do not always combine in the same proportion. If they are perfectly

pure and if, also, they combine in the most natural equilibrium, then the product is the most perfect of metals, namely
gold. Defects in purity or proportion or both result in the
formation of silver, lead, tin, or copper."[79] Now it is quite
apparent that, in the natural process of forming metallic
substances in the earth, two actions are necessary: namely,
heating and mixing. If *to temper* may be defined as "To
bring (anything) to a proper or suitable condition . . . by
mingling with something else,"[80] then Milton cannot be
wrong when he says that the stars *temper* all things that
grow and that the Sun's light *mixes* with terrestrial humor.
We may conclude that, in the generation of metals and gems,
the Sun's rays furnish heat necessary for the warming and
awakening of seminal virtues and their *"Extractions into
various* and *visible Forms"*;[81] as Paracelsus says, the Sun "is
the Vulcan of heaven accomplishing coction in the earth."[82]
And the elixir-produced corpuscles of potable gold, with
which the Sun's light is charged, are responsible for the
tempering of earthly substances and for their subjection to
mixture with astral virtues and powers. There can be no
doubt that, in the production of colorful and rare metals
and gems in the earth, the Sun's complex beams serve as
efficient cause.

In conclusion, one may observe with awe how Milton's
Sun dominates and controls all functions of the physical
universe and by what means his Lordship is established and
maintained. "His going forth is from the end of the heaven,
and his circuit unto the ends of it; and there is nothing hid
from the heat thereof." Planets and stars, impelled by his
magnetic beams, dance about him singing praises to his
power. The arch-chemic's divine Light, laden with solar

corpuscles of potable gold, circulates through the universe, tempers seminal virtues in the earth, and by mixture with terrestrial humors awakens all life and produces everything that grows. His Lordship, endowed with the Father's vice-geral dignity and energies transmitted through the Son, is thus established in majesty as "of this great world both eye and soul."

Chapter 6

I

THIS CHAPTER HAS SOMETHING TO SAY ABOUT CON-
cepts of the absolute Infinity of God or his attributes,
hyperbolical infinitudes of time and space, the relationship
between Spirit and matter, about mental and visual perspectives, directions, and distances in Milton's *Paradise Lost.*
It is especially concerned with the wanderings and adven-
tures of Lucifer, already in Heaven called Satan. This pro-
tagonist of epic proportions requires in action a vast stage
which represents the whole sweep of created existences,
Heaven of Heavens, Hell, chaos, and the Cosmos or World.

Perhaps consideration of the stage in miniature may help
to clarify its true relation to God, whom Milton conceives
to be infinite Spirit. Though as pure Spirit he is in no sense
subject to ordinary concepts of space and time, we may
cognize him, as the mystics have done, as an infinity of Light
who "contains within" himself all created things. Thus:
"within" the infinity of Light there is emanated or actuated
a comparatively tiny bubble, as it were, of limited room

SOME TRAVELS OF SATAN
AND THE ROAD TO HELL

called space; this bubble is at first clouded by a distributed matter, an efflux from God, which must still glow by reason of the omnipresence of divine Light. If one should inquire about what is "outside" of the bubble, the answer must be, There is no "outside" of space; there is only an infinite, incorporeal Deity "in" whom all things exist. Milton does not understand how matter emanates from Spirit; he must accept that fact by faith. But he is sure that space with its content of matter is noninfinite; only God is Infinite.[1]

For purposes of epic grandeur, however, the poet expands in concept the total spacial reality to whatever hyperbolical infinitude may be desired or imaginable—short of the Infinity of God. Accordingly, in some sense, he may represent certain aspects of the space-continuum as "vast infinitude" (III, 711), as "immeasurable abyss" (VII, 211) or "boundless deep" (I, 177), a suggestion of extension so illimitable and vast as to be incalculable or inconceivable. But such are epic phrases and must not be taken literally. In hyperbolical language the grand stage is being prepared for one of the most colossal actions ever conceived.

Now God prepares the cloudy matter of his global space for creation, and chaos is the result of this activity. Somewhere within an upper segment of the space-sphere, perhaps not far from the zenith, he creates in time out of chaos materials, through the instrumentality of his Son, the Empyrean or Heaven of Heavens, a place of unimaginable light. As Milton says, "Out of this light it appears that pleasures and glories, and a kind of perpetual heaven, have emanated and subsist" (*DC.*, XV, 29). Its crystal floor, resting upon dark chaos beneath, does not occupy the whole base of the global segment. Light streaming from its walls clarifies and beats down the adjacent chaos into a sort of turbulent sea-surface, whose waves roll against the battlements of Heaven as upon a shore. The Empyrean landscape is somewhat analogous to that of Earth, though its extent is immeasurably more vast. And in the midst of it—i.e., near the center of the whole heavenly region—stands the Mount of God, capped with blinding light, the immediate dwelling-place of Deity. Heaven of Heavens has no sky; above its floor and its layer of "air," there is only the effulgence of Light. Thus on the summit of God's Mount the zenith of all space opens up, shades off, as it were, and melts into that infinity of Light which is God or in which God dwells and has dwelt from all eternity (III, 3-5).

On a certain "day" an imperial summons brings all the innumerable hosts of Heaven before the Almighty's flaming throne (V, 584 ff.). They come in multitudes from all the outlying regions and ends of Heaven to hear pronounced God's exaltation of his only Son (V, 600 ff.). In the "evening" they dispose themselves about the Mount and later disperse in bands over the contiguous wide plain, "and wider far," Raphael reports, "Than all this globous earth in plain outspread" (V, 648-649). Of such imaginatively suggested vastness are the Courts of God. The Archangel Lucifer revolts in envy and pride and, as Satan, drawing a third of the angelic hosts about him, prepares to march homeward into Quarters of the North (V, 673 ff.).

It must be observed, then, that there are geographical directions in Heaven. Satan, standing at the foot of God's Mount and facing North, must know that on his left hand (i.e., to the West) there runs a broad and ample road— "whose dust is gold / And pavement stars"—leading from God's House in central Heaven to the blazing gateway in the western battlements (III, 500 ff.). Later the Son, returning victorious from creation of the World, goes eastward along this road until he reaches Heaven's high-seated top (VII, 577 ff.).

But Satan and his innumerable Powers march with winged speed northward. Here we are interested in the inexpressible distance covered overnight in their passage from the Mount of God in central Heaven to the region lying against the extreme northern battlements. Even Raphael has difficulty in making Adam understand the immense and almost inconceivable extension involved. Says he,

> Regions they passed, the mighty regencies
> Of seraphim and potentates and thrones
> In their triple degrees, regions to which
> All thy dominion, Adam, is no more
> Than what this garden is to all the earth,
> And all the sea, from one entire globose
> Stretched into longitude (V, 748-754).

Especially suggestive, as stimulus to the imagination, is the statement that elongation of a sphere—i.e., the globe of the

Earth—into a single line might indicate the distance covered before Satan reaches his native seat in the North. Returning Abdiel traverses this "wide champaign" of Heaven in a single night (VI, 1-2). And of Satan's celestial pursuers it is said: "so over many a tract / Of Heaven they marched, and many a province wide / Tenfold the length of this terrene" (VI, 76-77). They too come into the northern regions where the great battles occur. On the third day Messiah is victorious and, having expelled the rebels out of Heaven, he turns his chariot southward. In due time, celebrated by saints as sole victor, he rides "triumphant through mid heaven" into the courts of his mighty Father (VI, 888-890).

Meantime, Satan and his angels have been driven against the western wall of Heaven at some point in the extreme North. If the Empyreal bounds may be considered in the form of a square or "quadrature" (X, 381), then the point of expulsion lies somewhere in the western wall perhaps near its junction with the northern wall. If Heaven is circular in form—Milton is at one time uncertain whether it is square or round (II, 1048)—the expulsion point is situated in an arc of a circle so vast in circumference that one might question whether the segment were straight or curved. At any rate, the crystal wall of Heaven, open wide, rolls inward disclosing a spacious gate or gap overlooking the turbulent sea-surface of chaos (VI, 861 ff.). Rebellious angels observe with horror the wasteful Deep; but they are driven out, and "Disburdened heaven rejoiced, and soon repaired / Her mural breach, returning whence it rolled" (VI, 878-879). Now if one cares to view with eye of imagination the western wall of Heaven *from the outside,* he can see on his left hand the breached but repaired section of the crystal battlements, and on the right hand, at an almost inconceivable distance from the breach, the great western gateway of Heaven which opens upon the highway leading to God's Mount in the background.

From the breached wall of Heaven Satan and his hosts precipitate themselves downward through the wild anarchy of chaos. At times they are said to fall; but for the most part, since downward motion is not natural to them, they are pursued by eternal wrath (VI, 865), stricken with Heaven's afflicting thunder (II, 166), and compelled in laborious downward flight (II, 80) until yawning Hell receives them. However vast in extent the newly created universe of "bottomless" Hell may be, its flaming mouth is situated, approximately, directly beneath the breached western wall of Heaven. Though the time involved in the fall is only nine days (VI, 871), the distance from Heaven to Hell is literally immeasurable. It is the imaginative poet who places Hell "As far removed from God and light of Heaven / As from the center thrice to the utmost pole" (I, 73-74). This sort of measurement is, of course, merely symbolical and suggestive. As Professor Gilbert observes: "Milton has taken a unit of measurement that means *great beyond imagination* and has applied it to Chaos."[2]

Satan's return journey from Hellmouth to the newly created Mundane Universe must be considered in two sections. The first leg of his journey is upward and through noisy confusion of the hoary Deep, "a dark / Illimitable ocean, . . . / . . . where length, breadth, and height, / And time and place are lost" (II, 891-894). Here he finds at times a crude consistence of chaotic materials, bogs rough, dense, or rare, over and through which he swims, or sinks, or wades, or creeps, or flies; sometimes he falls in complete vacuity and is hurled aloft by explosion of some cloud instinct with fire and niter. It may seem strange that, in circumstances where there is no direction, he should have maintained in general a direct upward motion. It was Moloch who explained to Satan that ascent through chaos would be easy, because, says he, "in our proper motion we ascend / Up to our native seat: descent and fall / To us is adverse" (II, 75 ff.). But Satan does not find the ascent easy. With great difficulty he arrives at the pavilion of Chaos and sable-vested Night, who keep residence here upon the frontiers of their dark and chaotic realm. He inquires the readiest path which leads to where their "gloomy bounds / Confine with Heaven." Chaos, recognizing him, remembers how he and his numerous host recently passed this way with ruin on ruin, pursued by millions of victorious bands poured through the breached western wall of Heaven (II, 975 ff.). Satan learns that he is not far from the light which streams from the Empyreal battlements and that God has indeed created a new world. He rejoices that his sea of chaos should now find a shore, and

> With fresh alacrity and force renewed
> Springs upward like a pyramid of fire
> Into the wild expanse, and through the shock
> Of fighting elements, on all sides round
> Environed wins his way (II, 1011 ff.).

At last light appears from the walls of Heaven, reducing the tumult and hostile din of chaos and so sublimating its substance that he floats calmly in an atmosphere resembling air and at leisure beholds the wall of Heaven extended wide. His journey upward through chaos is now complete. It is clear that, whatever divagations may have characterized his recent flight, his upward motion has in general been along a straight line extending from Hellmouth, through chaos, past the pavilion of Chaos and Old Night, up to a point near that breach in Heaven's wall through which he and his followers were expelled.

Here the second leg of Satan's journey begins. Looking southward along the western wall of Heaven, he beholds in the distance the recently created Mundane Universe, pendant, linked in a golden chain to that side Heaven whence he and his legions fell (II, 1005-1006). He will learn later that it is suspended directly underneath the great western Gate (III, 500 ff.). But from his present vantage point the hanging World, viewed from an incalculable distance, seems "in bigness as a star / Of smallest magnitude close by the moon" (II, 1052-1053). Milton, of course, knows nothing about measuring distances in terms of light-years. But, as we have seen, he has already measured, in highly poetic language, the approximately parallel distance within the walls of Heaven. Keeping in sight his distant goal, Satan flies southward along the wall of Heaven, horizontally (with respect to Heaven), over the turbulent sea of chaos below. Or as God, looking down from his Mount, says to his Son,

> And now,
> Through all restraint broke loose he wings his way
> Not far off heaven, in the precincts of light,
> Directly towards the new created world (III, 86-89).

Meanwhile, the hieing Fiend, bent on revenge, alights and walks upon the outmost opacous globe of the round World. He discovers that this shell—which protects the luminous interior from the inroads of Darkness—is partly suspended in wild chaos. And whereas, viewed from afar, it appeared a globe—"a star of smallest magnitude"—it now seems a "boundless continent" (III, 422-423) vexed with ever-threatening and blustering storms. As he wanders upward along the surface of this vast expanse, he is sensitive to some glimmerings of light from above and, presently, comes to the brilliantly lighted zenith of the globe. Far distant, he descries a magnificent stairway leading up to the richly adorned western Gate of Heaven. And directly beneath, an orifice in the global structure permits a passage through the starry orbs down to Earth. He descends and finally arrives at the blissful seat of Paradise where he pursues his nefarious plan.

II

In Book II of *Paradise Lost* it is announced that Sin and Death, following Satan's track, paved a broad way from Hell to the outmost orb of this frail World (II, 1024 ff.). And in Book X are presented certain circumstantial details regarding the design, purposes, and building of so tremendous a structure. The distances to be spanned are incalculable; the obstacles to be met are almost insurmountable. But we may be sure that the great highway must, as was the case in Satan's journey, be considered and established in two sections: one leg leading like a tunnel upward through chaos to the dimly lighted frontiers of Chaos and Old Night, and another leg built like a bridge from that point over and above the roaring sea of chaos off the coast of Heaven to the outer sphere of the World.

But, one may ask, how are Sin and Death enabled to pursue the track of Satan? Sin, incestuous daughter of the Fiend, is impelled by an inexplicable attraction and instinct to follow her father-lover. She feels wings growing, she

says, and is conscious of new strength within her which may
give large dominion beyond the Deep. She is drawn by

Or sympathy, or some connatural force
Powerful at greatest distance to unite
With secret amity things of like kind
By secretest conveyance (X, 243 ff.).

With the help of her ill-begotten son, Death, and lest their
father find it impossible to return quickly over and through
the "Impassable" and "impervious" gulf (X, 254), she will
found a path from Hell to the new World. Death is eager to
aid; he scents carnage afar off, snuffs the smell of mortal
change on Earth, and tastes the savor of death from all
things that live there (X, 267-281). So equipped with instinct and powerful sense of smell, they proceed to their
great work.

Their process of construction is in some sense a minor
"creation," because they too reduce to order immense vol-
umes of chaotic materials. They fly out from Hellmouth
into the anarchy of chaos, gather available solid or slimy
matter, and crowd it to the mouth of Hell. There Death
smites into solidity the aggregated soil with his petrifying
mace, "the rest his look / Bound with Gorgonian rigor not
to move, / And with asphaltic slime" (X, 296-298). In this
manner they establish firmly a sort of pier in Hellmouth, and
as broad, which sustains one end of the upward-tending
causeway. But first the broad way is extended to the roots
of Hell itself (X, 280-299).

Little is reported about the construction of the road from
Hell through chaos up to light. Presumably even Milton
finds it almost impossible, or at least inexpedient, to describe
the building of such a passage through middle Darkness.

But that the completed work is in the form of a tunnel there can be no doubt. Later Satan, returning from Earth to Hell, passes along this way. He approaches Hellmouth on this last leg of his downward journey with complete comfort and safety while

> on either side
> Disparted chaos over built exclaimed,
> And with rebounding surge the bars assailed,
> That scorned his indignation (X, 415-418).

Now *dispart* is a violent term. One gets the impression that Sin and Death—they are very powerful (X, 284)—have opened up a wide passage through chaos by cleaving, forcing asunder, or causing to fly apart its conflicting elements. But unlike Satan who also forced his way through, they have stabilized their passage by the process of overbuilding it with unassailable bars. On either side, i.e., on each and every side, an indignant chaos violently surges against it in vain. One may hear the clamor and roar of attacking and rebounding chaos. But it is scarcely possible to represent except in concept or to discern, even with the eye of imagination, a perfectly black tunnel running through complete darkness. Consequently, Milton fixes his attention primarily, and for a special purpose, upon the building and appearance of the second section of the road from Hell to the World.

After the construct emerges into the precincts of light— not far from the breached wall of Heaven—it turns southward and becomes an immense mole spanning the sea-surface of chaos below. Still following Satan's track, Sin and Death "Paved after him a broad and beaten way / Over the dark abyss, whose boiling gulf / Tamely endured a bridge of wondrous length" (II, 1026-1028). It is now a causeway built high-arched "Over the foaming deep" (X, 300), "a ridge of pendent rock / Over the vexed abyss" (X, 313-314). And finally Sin and Death bring this work, wrought by "wondrous art pontifical," to the bare outside of this round World. They make it fast with pins of adamant and chains to the very spot where Satan landed safe from out of chaos. Thence the highway leads up to the zenith of the World's outside shell where an opening gives access to the interior.

Here "at the brink of chaos, near the foot / Of this new wondrous pontifice" (X, 347-348) Satan, returning from Paradise, meets his exultant offspring, Sin and Death. Satan rejoices "at sight / Of that stupendous bridge" (X, 350-351); Sin is glad that she has been able to "overlay / With this portentous bridge the dark abyss" (X, 370-371). Now appears clearly Milton's artistic purpose in emphasizing at length in Book X the construction and appearance of this visible bridge over chaos, some identical aspects of which he had briefly noted in Book II. He is especially interested here in the meeting at this point of three symbolical ways: one leading up to Heaven-gate, a stairway, each tread of which is "mysteriously . . . meant" (III, 516), one passing down to Earth, and one giving easy access to Hell. Satan, as he stands facing the battlements of Heaven, is able to observe all three of them at their junction, for

> now in little space
> The confines met of empyrean heaven
> And of this world, and on the left hand hell
> With long reach interposed; three several ways
> In sight, to each of these three places led (X, 320-324).

The triumphant Prince of Darkness enthusiastically approves of the road which stretches, on his "left hand, with

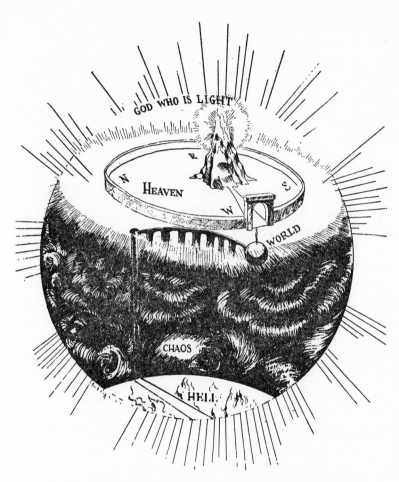

A DIAGRAM SUGGESTING THE RELATIONSHIP BETWEEN
GOD, WHO IS INFINITE LIGHT, AND TOTAL SPACE WITH
ITS CONTENT OF EMANATED AND CREATED REALITY

long reach interposed," down to Hell. By means of this
glorious work, he says, the Infernal Empire has been unified
with the new World into "one realm, one continent / Of
easy thoroughfare" (X, 391-394). Sin and Death are commanded to descend through the stars right down to Paradise,
where they are to dwell and reign in bliss; thence they will
exercise dominion over all the Earth, in the air and chiefly
on Man (X, 397-401). He himself descends "down / The
causey" (X, 414-415) and finally "through darkness" (X,
394) to Hell-gate. Meanwhile, good angels ascend and descend the celestial stairway or pass down to Earth, bent on
the execution of God's high behests. Thus the meeting of
three ways at the World's zenith is of tremendous importance in the poet's epic design; here are made "visible" the
roadways to three universes henceforth involved in the
struggle for the soul of Man.[3]

In this manner, it seems to me, Milton has established
and prepared for furnishing the vast stage upon which is
enacted the epic conflict between good and evil. The space-
continuum, limited though hyperbolically boundless, contains all emanated and created existences—Heaven, Hell,
chaos, and the World—and is itself "contained" in that
unique Infinity which is God. All creations and therefore
all movements are accomplished in some conceived "time,"
but all times are swallowed up in that "abyss, / Eternity,
whose end no eye can reach" (XII, 555-556). Satan's wanderings cover amazing stretches of hyperbolical infinitudes—
infinitudes which may be said to represent the expanded
universe of Milton's mind. And distances, expanses, directions, and perspectives are presented with such clarity and
poetic suggestiveness that one may well stand in awe of the
creative imagination which conceived them.[4]

Chapter 7

I

RAPHAEL IN MILTON'S PARADISE LOST EXPLAINS TO
Adam that angels of all ranks require food for the
sustenance of their bodies. For, says he, these pure intelligential substances, like the rational man, have within them
every lower faculty of sense, whereby they hear, see, smell,
touch, taste, and tasting concoct, digest, and assimilate. As
pure Spirits they are capable of transubstantiating easily the
gross corporeal viands of earth into an ethereal substance—
called incorporeal because of its purity—which sustains their
subtle and highly sublimated material bodies. Adam is impressed by the radiant form of his visitor and, somewhat
embarrassed, asks for further information. Whereupon, the
archangel proceeds to discourse upon the metaphysical relationship between men and angels, between all created
things and God:

> O Adam, one almighty is, from whom
> All things proceed, and up to him return,
> If not depraved from good, created all

MILTON'S SCALE OF NATURE

Such to perfection, one first matter all,
Endued with various forms, various degrees
Of substance, and, in things that live, of life;
But more refined, more spiritous, and pure,
As nearer to him placed or nearer tending
Each in their several active spheres assigned,
Till body up to spirit work, in bounds
Proportioned to each kind. So from the root
Springs lighter the green stalk, from thence the leaves
More airy, last the bright consummate flower
Spirits odorous breathes: flowers and their fruit
Man's nourishment, by gradual scale sublimed
To vital spirits aspire, to animal,
To intellectual, give both life and sense,
Fancy and understanding, whence the soul
Reason receives, and reason is her being,
Discursive, or intuitive; discourse
Is oftest yours, the latter most is ours,
Differing but in degree, of kind the same. . . .
                    time may come when men
With angels may participate, and find

No inconvenient diet, nor too light fare:
And from these corporal nutriments perhaps
Your bodies may at last turn all to spirit,
Improved by tract of time, and winged ascend
Ethereal, as we (V, 469-499).

And this series of relationships, set from center to circumference, Adam calls "the scale of nature."

Now, the surprising concept in this passage is not that the angels have bodies. Though the majority opinion of the Renaissance holds that spirits and daemons are pure intellectual substances unattached to vitalized forms,[1] still Milton is supported in his view by an honorable tradition involving the pronouncements of ancient Jews and the Pythagoreans as reported by Hierocles, of Plato, Apuleius, Plotinus, Psellus, St. Augustine and other Church Fathers, and of such contemporaries as Henry More and Ralph Cudworth.[2] Angels and daemons with fiery or aery or luciform or ethereal bodies are commonplace. What is surprising and significant is Milton's conception that the bodies of angels and the bodies of men and all other created things are formed out of the *same*, originally homogeneous matter, and that the composition of matter and material form is found not only in the material world but also in all spiritual substances. Also commonplace is the idea of a hierarchy of forces or powers or categories extending from God to Nature and through all the manifestations of Nature. Platonists and Scholastics had emphasized the position of the human spirit in this scale of Nature, and had shown how the spirit might climb the ladder to God—usually at the expense of the body. Somewhat startling, however, is the Miltonic doctrine that the moral disposition of the human spirit determines the corresponding purity or grossness of its material body, and that by means of moral virtue and obedience to God's laws

the body of man may at last turn all to spirit or may be sublimated to the point of becoming ethereal like the bodies of
angels. These distinguishing concepts of the composition
of matter and form in spiritual as well as material substances,
the creation of all things out of one homogeneous matter,
and the ability of the human spirit to form a suitable body
precisely adapted to its degree of purity are characteristic
of Milton, but they are not entirely original with him. It is
therefore the purpose of this chapter to develop, without
special emphasis upon immediate sources, the philosophical
traditions upon which in the presentation of these doctrines
he depends and so to furnish the basis for, possibly, a better
understanding of Raphael's metaphysical discourse.

But first it seems advisable to determine the precise significance of certain terms which the poet here employs.
When he asserts that angels assimilate food of an earthly
nature and so "corporeal to incorporeal turn" (V, 413), he
does not mean that gross matter is transformed into an entirely immaterial substance or into one having no bodily or
material structure. In this instance "incorporeal" has reference to a sublimed, tenuous, subtile matter like that which
composes the bodies of angels. As Origen says: "The term
. . . incorporeal is disused and unknown, not only in many
other writings, but also in our own Scriptures; . . . but . . .
it must be understood to mean that He [Christ] had not
such a body as demons have, which is naturally fine [sub-
tile], and thin as if formed of air (and for that reason is
either considered or called by many incorporeal), but that
He had a solid and palpable body. Now, according to
human custom, everything which is not of that nature is
called by the simple or ignorant incorporeal."[3] Johannes
Thessalonicensis agrees: "If you find angels, or demons, or
separate souls, called sometimes incorporeal, you must un-

derstand this in respect of the tenuity of their bodies only; as not consisting of the grosser elements, nor being so solid . . . as those, which we are now imprisoned in."[4] And Psellus generalizes as follows: "It is usual both with Christian writers, and Pagans too, to call the grosser bodies corporeal, and those, which, by reason of their subtilty, avoid both our sight and touch, incorporeal."[5] That Milton had some such concept in mind is indicated by the fact that, when the hungry Raphael—not seemingly the angel, nor in mist (the common gloss of theologians)—transubstantiates corporeal food into incorporeal, this easy process is compared to that of the alchemist who transmutes drossiest ore into perfect gold (V, 433-442).

This "incorporeal" body of the angel, moreover, is composed of ether. Milton asserts that (1) angels are spirits, and (2) that they are of ethereal nature (DC., XV, 35). And Raphael holds out to Adam the hope that some day the human body may turn all to spirit and "winged ascend ethereal," as the angels. Here it is necessary to understand that Milton is not following that tradition which conceives of ether as a fifth essence differing in kind from all the four elements. He holds rather to the historical theory that ether is a matter sublimated from the four elements, or merely a purer form of air and fire.[6] Both the visible and invisible heavens, therefore, the bodies of planets, stars, and angels, are composed of a thin, attenuated, purified form of that same matter which metaphysically underlies all other created things. Thus a material continuity is established between the invisible and visible worlds, where one first matter is more or less refined, spiritous, and pure in proportion as it exists nearer to God or farther away from him (V, 470-479). When therefore Raphael says that Adam's body may "at last turn all to spirit," no one must suppose that "spirit" is here to be taken in the sense of an immaterial being or intelligence conceived as distinct from anything physical or material.[7] He simply means that Adam's body may, before the fall, be refined and purified into an ethereal body like that of a Spirit or angel.

Milton's conception of one first matter, derived from God and endued with various forms, various degrees of substance and of life,[8] may be found to have distinguished theological and philosophical support. Long before him Origen, in his discussion of the human spirit's condition after death,[9] had maintained the thesis that all rational and spiritual natures— with the exception of the Trinity alone—must always be united to bodies. Says he: "The necessity of logical reasoning compels us to understand that rational natures were indeed created at the beginning, but that material substances were separated from them only in thought and understanding, and appears to have been formed for them, or after them, and that they never have lived nor do live without it."[10] And in explanation of the apparent diversity found in the bodies of angels, stars, and of men in various states, he is forced to postulate a universal matter or bodily nature which "admits of diversity and variety of change, so that it is capable of undergoing all possible transformations," possessing such "properties as to enable it to be sufficient for all the bodies in the world which God willed to exist."[11] He concludes:

As we have remarked above, therefore, that material substance of this world, possessing a nature admitting of all possible transformations, is, when dragged down to beings of a lower order, moulded into the crasser and more solid condition of a body, so as to distinguish those visible and varying forms of the world; but when it becomes the servant of more perfect and more blessed beings, it shines in the splendour of celestial bodies, and adorns either the angels of God or the sons of the resurrection with the clothing of a spiritual body, out of all which will be filled up the diverse and varying state of the one world.[12]

Here one may observe a hierarchy of spiritual and rational natures clothed at the beginning with a variety of material bodies formed from a single bodily nature, from one matter precisely adapted to the degree of life with which it is endued. It is the Creator who adorns the angels and the sons of the resurrection with the clothing of a spiritual body; he purifies matter so that it shines in the splendor of the celestial bodies, and he drags it down to form the crass bodies of beings of a lower order, such as men. But here is only slight suggestion of the ability lodged in a vital human spirit to transform its gross body into a spiritual or ethereal body like that of angels.

A more systematic account of a homogeneous matter which supports all created things may be found in the *Fons Vitae* of Avencebrol.[13] This Jewish philosopher, combining certain elements of Aristotelian and Neoplatonic speculation, conceives of the created universe as the product of a constantly deteriorating emanation. First, there subsists an absolutely unified, simple, and unknowable God (III, 11-12). From him as Creator comes the World Spirit, an Intelligence which is composed of universal matter (*materia universalis*) and universal form (*forma universalis*),[14] the compound being effected by the will of God.[15] From this Intelligence proceeds a gradually weakening or degenerating succession of inferior intelligences (also composed of matter and form), which transmit the hylomorphic principle of substantial composition into the material world. Thus a hierarchy of forms successively differentiate *materia universalis* into a graduated and infinite variety of spiritual and corporal beings. Or to state the case differently, any individual thing will represent a plurality of forms rooted in the *forma universalis* and a multiplicity of matters differentiated from a numerically one *materia universalis*.[16] Concerning these two universal principles Avencebrol says that a definition is impossible, but he may attempt a description: "ergo descriptio materiae primae, quae sumpta est ex eius proprietate, haec est, scilicet quod est substantia existens per se, substintatrix diversitatis, una numero; et iterum describitur sic, quod est substantia receptibilis omnium formarum. sed descriptio formae universalis haec est, scilicit quod est substantia constituens essentiam omnium formarum; et iterum describitur sic, quod ipsa est sapientia perfecta, lumen purissimum."[17] And the various matters of creation—all degrees of which are ultimately reducible to one matter (IV, 15)—are more pure and subtile in proportion as they are differentiated by the light of forms when it is close to its original source, and they become more gross, dense, and turbulent as the light extends farther away from God.[18] It is therefore clear that the matter of intelligences—identified by later Christian writers with angels—is merely a nobler, more simple and sublime species of that same *materia universalis* which is differentiated into the bodies of men. As Thomas Aquinas says:

Some assert that the angels are composed of matter and form; which opinion Avicebron endeavoured to establish in his book of the *Fount of Life*. For he supposes that whatever things are distinguished by the intellect are really distinct. Now as regards incorporeal substance, the intellect apprehends that which distinguishes it from corporeal substances, and that which it has in common with it. Hence he concludes that what distinguishes incorporeal from corporeal substance is a kind of form to it, and whatever is subject to this distinguishing form, as it were something common, is its matter. Therefore, he asserts, the universal matter of spiritual and corporeal things is the same; so that it must be understood that the form of incorporeal substance is impressed in the matter of spiritual things, in the same way as the form of quantity is impressed in the matter of corporeal things.[19]

That Milton is acquainted with this concept of a multiplicity of matters differentiated from one prime or universal matter by a plurality of generic and individual forms cannot be doubted. In the *Logic* he speaks of "*A thing:* that is the thing which the matter makes evident, to wit, the effect produced by the matter, since we know that matter is common to all entities and nonentities, not peculiar to sensible and corporeal things. But of whatever sort these things are, such the matter of them ought to be; the sensible should be composed of sensible things, the eternal of eternal things, and so on in the rest" (51, 53). And again (*ibid.*, 59) he says: "Because if whatever things differ in number differ also in essence, but not in matter, necessarily they differ among themselves in forms, but not in common forms, therefore in proper ones. Thus the rational soul is the form of man generically; the soul of Socrates is the proper form of Socrates." One might safely conclude, it seems to me, that it is Avencebrol's conception of a plurality of forms and matters rooted in a *materia universalis*—initiated by the distinguished Jew—which constitutes the ultimate source of the Miltonic postulation of

> one first matter all,
> Endued with various forms, various degrees
> Of substance, and, in things that live, of life;
> But more refined, more spiritous, and pure,
> As nearer to him placed or nearer tending.

But the channels through which these distinctive ideas were transmitted from Avencebrol to Milton are not clearly defined.

Still it is instructive to observe that in the Middle Ages Avencebrol exerted a stimulating influence and that certain aspects of his system were popular, particularly among philosophers of the Franciscan school. Among the older Scholastics Alexander of Hales, for example, supports the hylomorphic theory of substantial composition in all contingent beings, spiritual as well as material. But his three matters— spiritual, celestial corporeal, and terrestrial corporeal—are not differentiated from one common matter and are therefore different in kind.[20] For St. Bonaventura, likewise, all things are composed of matter and form, and he seems to recognize the existence of a homogeneous matter underlying all material bodies and spiritual beings.[21] But it is Duns Scotus who openly avows his dependence upon the principles of Avencebrol. Following the Jewish philosopher he postulates three species or varieties of matter: *materia primo prima, materia secundo prima,* and *materia tertio prima.* C. R. S. Harris has defined these concepts admirably:

Materia primo prima is the common substrate of all created beings. It is that which is absolutely indeterminate with regard to all forms whatsoever, and its actuality is infinitesimal; it is only just removed from nothing, possessing in its essence neither substantial nor accidental form which determines it to be anything in particular, its only reality being that which it receives immediately from God as the product of his creative act. It possesses less entity than any other creature, . . . and is therefore ontologically prior to all its determinations.

Materia secundo prima is that which is the substratum of generation and corruption, coming to being and passing away. It is that which is transformed by created agents, i.e. the forces of nature. It differs from *materia primo prima* in that it is already informed with some substantial form by virtue of which it is quantitatively determined, and therefore susceptible of physical changes like growth and decay, &c.

Materia tertio prima is the matter of every particular natural agent, as for instance, the seed of the oak. . . . It includes also the material of the arts.[22]

As indicated Duns would insist not only upon the existence of matter in all created substances, material and spiritual, but also upon the unity and homogeneity of this matter. Since the universe is a unity, everything that exists must be rooted in *materia primo prima*. As Harris concludes: "Finally, where we find objects specifically or numerically determined arising out of the indeterminate we say that they partake of a common matter. Thus, for example, we make the assumption concerning the four elements, which we regard as the differentiation of one prime matter . . . we conclude that all things arise out of the differentiation of one common indeterminate matter, which is differentiated by the various generic and specific forms into the various creatures, angels, heavenly bodies, terrestrial bodies, and so forth."[23] And most significant for us here, Duns likens the created universe to a wonderful tree: "Ex his apparet, quod mundus est arbor quaedam pulcherrima, cujus radix et seminarium est materia prima, folia fluentia sunt accidentia; frondes et rami sunt creata corruptibilia; flos, rationalis anima; fructus naturae consimiles et perfectionis, natura Angelica. . . . Dividitur radix ista immediate in duos ramos, in corporalem et spiritualem; spiritualis ramus in tres hierarchias, et quaelibet illarum in tres ordines, et ordo quaelibet in millia millium Angelorum. . . . Corporalis creatura duos

ramos continet, scilicet corpora corruptibilia et incorrupti-
bilia, et illa dividuntur multipliciter."[24]

Now it may be apparent that in some way Milton is acquainted with certain elements of Duns' system and perhaps
with his metaphorical expression. For example, the poet
too recognizes three states or varieties or divisions of matter.
In the *Logic* (53) he observes: "Matter is commonly divided into primary and secondary; the secondary into proximate and remote." These distinctions are especially useful
in Physics and he, as logician, is interested in only proximate
matter, such as that which constitutes the matters of the arts.
But it is clear that his primary matter—his one first matter
from which all things are created—corresponds precisely in
all respects to Duns' *materia primo prima* and is, like the
latter, ontologically prior to all its differentiations. His remote matter—a division of secondary matter—corresponds to
Duns' *materia secundo prima*. And this "remote" matter is
the substance of chaos in *Paradise Lost*, which, like the *materia secundo prima,* is the substrate of generation and corruption; in chaos prime matter is already differentiated into
the four elements and has acquired quantity and extension.
Moreover, in the symbol of the tree Milton seems to be suggesting certain metaphysical relationships identical with
those which Duns presents through the same image. The
poet has just informed us that all things are created from
one first matter endued with a variety of forms and that a
more refined species of this matter is to be found clothing
those spiritual forms placed nearer to God. He continues:

> So from the root
> Springs lighter the green stalk, from thence the leaves
> More airy, last the bright consummate flower
> Spirits odorous breathes: flowers and their fruit.

The artist, of course, merely suggests rather than states the
details of a parallelism obtaining between the tree and a
unified world created out of one prime matter; he is mainly
interested in the higher manifestations of bodily and spiritual development. But it is evident in the comparison that
the root of the tree is prime matter, the green stalk and the
leaves constitute the corruptible creation (including perhaps
the vital and animal spirits of living creatures), the flower
is the intellectual or rational soul of man, and the fruit is
the rational-intuitive soul of angels.[25]

Thus far Milton and Duns, like Origen, have given a clear
exposition of a hierarchy of forms combined with a graduated series of matters differentiated from one matter. Here
is presented the concept of, shall we say, a static and complete universe as God originally created it, comprising all
creatures of high or low estate, "Each to their several active
spheres assigned, / . . . in bounds / Proportioned to each
kind." But now Milton proceeds to introduce the new doctrine—alien to Duns and Avencebrol—of a dynamic force or
power which is able to overleap the bounds proportioned to
its kind and attain a sphere to which it was not originally
assigned. The flowers—and their fruit—of the metaphorical
tree suggest a reintroduction of the main proposition concerning the nourishment which is necessary for the support
of human and angelic bodies. He observes that man is able
by vital processes to sublimate the fruit of trees to sensitive
and animal spirits, thence to intellectual, whence the soul
receives discursive reason. And since angels differ from man
in degree of perfection only and not in kind, they too are
able to receive gross nutriment and convert it to their proper
substance. These considerations lead to the conclusion that
in time the purified spirits of men may achieve the conversion of their crass bodies into an ethereal substance like that

which is formed into the bodies of angels. This dynamism, involving both physical and spiritual development, reaches Milton through channels other than those which we have discussed.

II

Two schools of Neoplatonic thinkers elaborate the thesis that the human spirit is of such a nature that it is capable of determining the state of its body. Both agree that the soul of man is a rational or spiritual substance which pre-existed before its lapse into an earthly body, and that at its first creation it was provided with an ethereal, celestial integument called the luminous or luciform body. One school holds that this chariot or vehicle of the soul adheres to it always and that it descends with the soul into the earthly body, where it serves as a unifying and vitalizing principle between the two. Hierocles, for example, attributed this concept to the Pythagoreans. Says he,

The rational Essence having receiv'd from God its Creator a Body conformable to its Nature, descended hither upon Earth, so that 'tis neither a Body, nor without a Body; but being incorporeal it has nevertheless its Form determin'd and bounded by the Body; Even as in the Stars. . . . 'Tis the same with all rational Essences, as well with the Heroes as with Men; for a Hero is a rational Soul with a luminous Body; and Man is likewise a rational Soul with an immortal Body created with it. Thus you see the Doctrine of *Pythagoras*, which *Plato* in his *Phaedrus* explain'd long after him, comparing the divine Soul and the human Soul to a wing'd Chariot, that has two Horses and a Coachman to guide it.[26]

Now the Purity here spoken of, extends . . . to the whole Management and Usage of our mortal Body, in which is lodg'd our luminous Body, which inspires Life into the inanimate Body, and contains and preserves all its Harmony. For the immaterial body is the Life, and produces the Life of the material Body; by which Life our mortal Body becomes perfect, being compos'd of the immaterial Life, and of the material Body.[27]

But when the incorporeal soul falls through folly into a terrestrial body, the luciform vesture which clothes it is dimmed and its splendor (as a light in a dark lantern) is weakened and obscured by the gross weight and passions of the earthly body. Hierocles therefore recommends (1) the purgation of man's rational soul by means of mathematical science and dialectics, and (2) the purification of the luminous body through contemplation, proper diet, and the practice of magical or ceremonial arts. Thus purged and purified the rational soul and its lucid body may slough off entirely the gross earthly body and winged, may attain their pristine splendor in the pure ether.[28] Thus in one branch of Neoplatonic philosophy, stemming avowedly from the ancient Pythagoreans, we discover among other considerations one significant core of thought: namely, the celestial body of the rational soul may lose its brightness and fall through the soul's folly and may regain its original glory through the practice of virtue. But the respective substances of the earthly body and of the luciform body are different in kind, and there is no possibility that one may be transubstantiated into the other.

Another school of Neoplatonists, however, are of the opinion that the human soul, according to its moral state, always finds or creates for itself a cognate body correspondingly refined or gross. Thus when the soul descends into the material world, its celestial body is lost and it acquires an earthy body; but the celestial body may be regained through the exercise of virtue. As Porphyry says: "However the soul be in itself affected, so does it always find a body suitable and agreeable to its present disposition; and therefore to the

purged souls does naturally accrue a body, that comes next
to immateriality; that is, an ethereal one."[29] It is not here
stated, we must observe, that the various bodies which the
soul creates for itself in its fall and rise are formed from the
same matter, more or less pure. But the dynamic power of
the soul to determine any present state of its body is firmly
established. Now it is not clear when this concept of a spiritual dynamism was first combined with that of a universal
prime matter, out of which all material and spiritual things
are created. Already Cornelius Agrippa, at any rate, seems
to imply such a combination when he describes mystically
how the "first light" of reason passes from God into man's
soul, hence through the vivifying celestial body into the elemental body, where the light is made manifestly visible to
the eye. He continues:

The *Chaldean* Philosophers considering this progress of light,
declare a certain wonderfull power of our mind: *viz* that it may
come to passe, that our mind being firmly fixed on God, may be
filled with the divine power; and being so replenished with light,
its beams being diffused through all the *media,* even to this
grosse, dark, heavy, mortall body, it may endow it with abundance of light, and make it like the Stars, and equally shining,
and also by the plenty of its beams and lightness lift it on high,
as straw lifted up by the flame of fire, and can presently carry
the body as a spirit into remote parts.[30]

And certainly by Milton's time the most distinguished philosophers were familiar with the idea of one universal, homogeneous matter and a dynamic human soul capable of forming it into a body of corresponding grossness or purity. Dr.
Henry More, for example, finds that "so far as either our
Sense or Reason can reach, there is the *same Matter* every
where. . . . For *Matter* being of one simple homogeneal nature, and not distinguishable by specificall differences, as

the Schools speak, it must have every where the very same Essentiall properties."[31]   And the human soul, by virtue of its ability to move and establish a "vital congruity" with this universal matter, may fashion for itself in successive states of existence a terrestrial, an aerial, and a celestial body.[32] Ralph Cudworth, identifying the spiritual body of the risen Christ as a purified form of the same numerical body which was laid in the sepulcher, generalizes: "According to the best philosophy, which acknowledges no essential or specifical differences of matter, the foulest and grossest body that is, merely by motion [of the spirit] may not only be crystalized, but also brought into the purity and tenuity of the finest ether."[33]   And Dean George Rust presents the opinions of Origen together with some rather startling Neoplatonic interpretations.[34]

Rust agrees with Origen that the Trinity alone is truly incorporeal and that all created essences are provided with bodies formed out of one universal matter.[35] He postulates a "long chain of life and Being," consisting of a hierarchy of spiritual substances incorporated in bodies of appropriate purity and extending from incorporeal Deity to matter itself. These graduated orders of spiritual essences—the souls of men constitute one order—were at first creation "joyned to the purest matter, and placed in the best Regions of the world that the highest life and purity of Essence they then had made them then fit for."[36] Thus we meet again the concept of a static universe as God originally created it, consisting of various orders of incorporate spirits assigned to their respective spheres in bounds proportioned to each kind. "But," says Rust, proceeding to develop the concept of a dynamism lodged in spiritual substances, "since few Spirits after the *First* and *Best* are of immutable purity, and since every different degree of their changeable purity is proportion'd to a correspondent degree of purity in matter, and since matter is actually existent in the world according to all degrees of purity, 'tis not to be wondered at neither that the same individual Spirit or some order of Spirits should be sometimes united with one sort of matter sometimes with another."[37] In this manner he would establish a basis for the observation that the preexistent soul of man may through folly descend the chain of life until it is plunged into a gross terrestrial body, and that it may through virtuous living ascend the scale until even the grossest vesture of decay may be transmuted into a "spiritual" body, *not only at the resurrection but here in this life.* For, says he, "to every remarkable difference of purity in the Essence of created Spirits there is a difference in matter exactly answering and fitted thereto, and by how much more pure they are, by so much more durable is their life, as approaching nearer to and more fully partaking of the first and purest fountain of life."[38]

For example, the soul of Christ was possessed of such sovereign energy and life that it "could as well fix and constipate the matter of his body into a terrestrial crassness, as loosen it into a spiritual tenuity." This was possible because of the fact that "there is no other difference in matter then what it receives from such or such modifications of its parts, and that it is capable of all these modifications where a sufficient cause works upon it." His transfigured body, therefore, molded into form and shape by the imagination and other natural powers of its actuating Spirit, could easily pass through such bodies as to others were impervious, and was at will not subject to the pull of gravity. He rarely exercised this power of the Spirit during his life upon earth. But after he had passed through death, his quickening Spirit subdued all that was mortal in him, broke through and melted his body into such rarity, tenuity, and fineness as would like a winged chariot carry him into the ethereal heavens.[39] Such spiritualized bodies human beings may expect to acquire at the resurrection. But most marvellous of all, since "that excellent and most *energetical* part in us which the Scripture calls *Spirit*, being thoroughly enlivened, hath a power to quicken any kinde of body it is united with into a vigour and subtilty answerable to its own might and purity," men may attain *in this life* a glorified body such as that of the transfigured or risen Christ. Observe that holy man, Elias; "the chariots of fire and horses of fire mentioned in the story of his ascension plainly signify to the intelligent reader in what kind of *vehicle* he ascended." Rust concludes: "And something like this may be said also of Elias; that he had attained in some sort to the *resurrection of the dead* in this life, which in the *Jewish* notion is the same with the *vivification of the body* (as is plain in many places in St. Paul's Epistles)."[40]

From the considerations presented above some might deduce the conclusion that Milton is an eclectic who slavishly reproduces in poetic form a conglomeration of speculations transmitted to him from ancient Pythagoreans and Chaldeans through early Neoplatonists, mediaeval Scholastics, and the Platonists of his time. The fact is, however, that Milton is no eclectic. He does indeed employ the concept, elaborated by Origen, Avencebrol, Duns Scotus, and others, of one homogeneous matter differentiated by a hierarchy of forms. His scale of Nature is not completely original with him. Moreover, he follows the Platonists in attributing to the human spirit the vital power of determining the state of its material body. But he also reads the sacred Scriptures and interprets them independently for himself. He will not therefore support the theory of preexisting souls—created in the beginning with or without bodies of any texture—who through their fault and negligence fell from their high estate and became inhabitants of the earth in terrestrial bodies. When God created man in his own image, says he, "it was not the body alone that was then made, but the soul of man also (in which our likeness to God principally consists)" (*DC.*, XV, 37, 39).

> God formed man of the dust of the ground,
> And breathed into his nostrils the breath of life;
> Thus man became a living soul.

Though the whole man into whose body God breathed the breath of life may thus be called a "living soul," still the animating spirit may be distinguished in thought from the material body (*DC.*, XV, 41, 43). And "unless we had rather take the heathen writers for our teachers respecting the nature of the soul," this breath of life infused into man "was not a portion of God's essence, or a participation of the divine nature, but that measure of the divine virtue or influence, which was commensurate to the capabilities of the recipient" (*DC.*, XV, 39). So Milton would conceive for the human spirit an origin different from that attributed to it by many contemporary thinkers.

III

Any adequate exposition of Milton's doctrine concerning the soul's origin must, it seems to me, emphasize the hylomorphic composition of all created things. "For," says he, "there is nothing that does not have its form, though unknown to us."[41] He holds it self-evident that *"Man consists of spirit and body,"* and that "the rational soul is the form of man, since through this man is man and is distinguished from all other natures."[42] What, then, is the proximate origin of the human soul considered as the form of the body? He does not leave us in doubt: "It is acknowledged by the common consent of almost all philosophers, that every *form,* to which class the human soul must be considered as belonging, is produced by the power of matter" (*DC.,* XV, 49). But from such a statement as this we must not conclude, with Saurat, that "for Milton all is matter, and spirit is only a more refined sort of matter,"[43] or with Masson, that "All created Being, whether called soul or body, consists of but one primordial matter."[44] Milton does not say that the human soul was produced from matter or that it consists of matter; he says precisely what he means, namely, that it was produced "by the power of matter." Matter *per se* is completely passive and has no power within itself to produce anything until it is prepared for the reception of forms by the efficient cause, who is God. Says Milton: "In the order of nature matter follows the efficient cause, and is a sort of effect of the efficient cause; for the efficient cause prepares the matter that it may be fit for receiving the form. As the efficient cause is that which first moves, so the matter is that which is first moved."[45] It is therefore evident that God, the efficient cause, has not only prepared from primary matter a remote-secondary matter fitted for the reception of forms, but has also communicated to it his divine virtue or influence, i.e., the forms of all created things. And the form thus communicated is the "power" of matter which produces the human soul. As Milton concludes: "There seems there-

fore no reason, why the soul of man should be made an
exception to the general law of creation. For . . . God
breathed the breath of life into other living beings, and
blended it so intimately with matter, that the propagation
and production of the human form were analogous to those
of other forms, and were the proper effect of that power
which had been communicated to matter by the Deity"
(DC., XV, 53).

In *Paradise Lost* Milton gives a graphic representation of
the manner in which God communicates forms to a prepared
matter, and reveals concretely how the "power of matter"
produces within six days all the creatures of the visible
world, including the spirit of man. Here, as we have said,
primary matter—produced originally as an emanation or efflux from the Deity, i.e., as the effect of a bodily power or
virtue subsisting within his spiritual Being (DC., XV, 21,
23)[46]—has already been differentiated into the four elements
by the power of God. This remote-secondary matter, called
chaos, is without definite bounds and dimensions; within its
"crude consistence" hot, cold, moist and dry strive tumul-
tuously for the mastery because they as yet represent neither
sea, nor shore, nor air, nor fire, "But all these in their pregnant causes mixed confusedly." The "dark materials" of this
chaos constitute the substrate of generation and corruption,
the womb of Nature and perhaps her grave (II, 890-940).
And it is this formless substance, this remote matter prepared by the efficient cause for the reception of forms, which
is "afterwards adorned and digested into order by the hand
of God" (DC., XV, 23). The process of adorning a selected
part of chaos with vitalizing forms—that is, the process of
creation—is dramatically represented. God conceives of the

cosmos and by an exercise of will executes his design through his power and virtue invested in his Son, the Word, who serves as executive agent. Thus the Word, accompanied by God's Spirit and might, rides with the hosts of Heaven into wildly surging chaos and with golden compasses establishes bounds to that portion of it which is to become the visible Universe. As Milton concludes:

> Thus God the heaven created, thus the earth,
> Matter unformed and void: Darkness profound
> Covered the abyss: but on the watery calm
> His brooding wings the spirit of God outspread,
> And vital virtue infused, and vital warmth
> Throughout the fluid mass, but downward purged
> The black tartareous cold infernal dregs
> Adverse to life: then founded, then conglobed
> Like things to like, the rest to several place
> Disparted, and between spun out the air,
> And earth, self balanced on her center hung (VII, 232-242).

And the creation of the visible Universe is instantaneous and complete.[47] The "vital virtue" and "vital warmth" which the Spirit infuses into matter constitute the forms of all things invested with the vital power of autonomous development. Here the Spirit of God—"that is," says Milton, "his divine power, rather than any person" (DC., XV, 13)—communicates to chaotic matter those creative powers or hidden seeds of things born corporeally—sometimes called "seminal reasons" or *logoi spermatikoi*—which are the pale reflections of exemplars in the mind of God.[48] Here we find "one first matter all, / Endued with various forms, various degrees / Of substance, and, in things that live, of life." Within the vitalized forms—manifestations not of divine essence but

merely of the might and virtue of the Deity—God has set
his commands for the unfolding of all things in the visible
world during the six days of creation. And having so invested the matter of the universe with his vitalizing power—
which fills all space as with a light—God as pure spiritual
essence retires from the material complex and allows it to
develop as he has commanded (VII, 169-172).[49] Still for
various reasons Milton employs the Biblical formula, "And
God said . . ."

On the sixth day, for example, God said, "Let the earth
bring forth soul[50] living in her kind." And the Earth, already
impregnated with the vital forms of every living thing,
obeys. Straightway out of the ground uprise beasts of the
field as from their lairs; the grassy clods calve, and broad
herds spring up; the lion paws himself free from the binding
earth; other animals, rising, throw the crumbled soil above
them; the stag bears up his branching head from underground; behemoth, biggest born of earth, heaves up his vastness. And now from this same Earth, so quickened by the
vital virtue of the Spirit of God, springs the chief of all natural creatures, man, endued with the sanctity of reason and
ordained to govern the rest. Self-knowing, he stands erect
and finds himself capable of directing worship and devotion
to God Supreme. Thus the rational spirit or form of man,
like the breath of life in other living creatures, is the effect
produced by that power which God communicated through
his Spirit to a prepared matter. When therefore on the sixth
day this form of man is intimately blended with matter, i.e.,
when God makes man out of the dust of the ground and
breathes into his nostrils the breath of life, Adam stands
forth as a complete "living soul."[50] In this manner Milton

would explain the divine origin of the human spirit as form of the body. But once the spirit is generated, he invests it with that same dynamism which Neoplatonists attribute to the preexistent souls of men.[51] Before the fall Adam is immortal; his obedient spirit may, in the lapse of time, sublimate his natural body to the texture of the angelic body, and he may dwell in Heaven or in Paradise as he pleases (V, 499-500).[52]

In conclusion, it must be observed that Milton's doctrine concerning the scale of nature represents a distinguished syncretism of elements derived from a variety of philosophical traditions. His reason and poetic imagination, working in harmony, fuse the Christian concept of an historical creation dependent upon the will of God with Neoplatonic speculations regarding the human spirit's power to determine the state of its material body. He embraces something like Augustinian exemplarism and combines it with the theory of a plurality of forms which differentiate one homogeneous matter into a multiplicity of appropriate matters. Thus the unity of all created things is established; the creatures of the visible and invisible worlds differ in degree of perfection but not in kind. This doctrine cannot be called "materialism," because active spiritual essences are consistently distinguished from the passive materials which they modify. It cannot be designated "pantheism," because God as pure spirit does not extend his divine nature or essence into the material world; he creates and supports by a communication of his virtue or power or influence. But since both visible and invisible creation is rooted in the propagation of a material cause or principle inherent in the spiritual Being of God, Milton's full concept of the scale of Nature may properly be called theopantism.[53]

EPILOGUE

Now (MILTON HAS APPARENTLY COMPLETED A STAGE OF sufficient immensity upon which he is enabled to present a sublime action asserting divine providence and purposing to justify the ways of God to men.) As ontologist he has approached the Being of Divinity and defined his essential properties together with the qualities of the Son and Holy Spirit; he has analyzed the essences of angels, of human beings, and of all created things, showing relationships of all secondary natures to each other and to God. As cosmogonist he has derived formless matter—the substrate of all creatures—from God who prepares it into a tumultuous chaos endowed with an appetite for forms. And as physicist Milton, a sort of atomist, has revealed in some detail the genesis of the World and all other creatures out of the prepared matter of chaos. Though the stage as thus conceived and executed is situated within the limits of total space, still it is not yet finished and will not be complete until vital alterations shall have been accomplished in the World's structure.

It is Michael who shows to Adam the whole course of human history as many tomorrows, hurrying to the last syllable of recorded time and lighting many generations of good and bad men to dusty death. And at the end of this racing time, what then? As Adam says, "beyond is all abyss, / Eternity, whose end no eye can reach." One may well falter in approaching even the precincts of eschatology. But having set my love upon the beauties of Milton's Mundane Universe and having visited his Heaven of Heavens, chaos, and Hell, I am impelled to make some inquiries regarding the ultimate end or fate of these ineffable entities. Solutions of this problem are infinitely difficult, partly because the arrangement of contents in Milton's total universe is different essentially from that of all others conceived and, mainly therefore, because no inspired prophecies of the Holy Scriptures regarding "last things" or surmises of theologians and others are precisely applicable to the predicament in *Paradise Lost*. Be that as it may, God foresees and Michael announces that, after the Millennium, the Son of God will return to Earth in glory to judge the quick and the dead. On this Judgment Day Satan and his rebel angels together with all evil men shall be cast into the fires of Hell, the doors of which shall be henceforth locked forever. Thus it is indicated that the structure of Milton's Hell and its means of torture must remain unaltered through eternity. On the other hand, Christ the Son shall, after judgment, mount into the Heaven of Heavens—as he vowed would be the case before he came first to Earth—accompanied by a multitude of his redeemed souls. For these he has no doubt already prepared mansions in accordance with his promise as revealed to St. John. By this time, then, the general tone, atmosphere, and to some extent appearance of the Heaven of Heavens will have been changed: here now no cloud of anger shall remain in God's face, peace and reconcilement after strife having been assured; mansions of redeemed saints not reared with hands shall contribute greatly to the splendor of those regions and to the universal bliss of Heaven's new inhabitants; joy and love and truth having triumphed, the Son shall lay aside his scepter, and God shall be All in All. It may be reasonably surmised, moreover, that chaos shall always serve as the foundation of Miltonic Heaven of Heavens and the basic source of its physical grandeurs. For matter is not likely to be annihilated, and with graduated forms it must exist forever as sustainer of created essences in both Heaven of Heavens and Hell.

In the Final Conflagration, however, Milton's Mundane Universe, like any cosmos conceived by Biblical writers, would seem destined to suffer perhaps complete dissolution and its original substances absorbed into chaos. From Isaiah to Revelation one may entertain fearful prophecies of how, at the coming of Christ, visible heaven and earth shall pass away and no place be found for them. On that terrifying day, it is said, the sun shall become black as sackcloth of hair, the moon red as blood; all the hosts of stars shall be dissolved and fall upon the earth; with a great noise heaven itself shall vanish away like smoke or as a scroll when it is rolled together. The earth, reserved unto fire against this day of judgment, shall also be dissolved: mountains and islands shall be shaken out of their places; the elements shall melt with fervent heat; the earth and all the works that are in it shall be burned up and remembered no more. Now Milton has thoughtfully conned such prophecies and in *The Christian Doctrine* has gathered many texts pertaining to the conflagrant event. With some hesitation and a shade of indifference he concludes: "Whether by this is meant the destruction of the substance of the world itself, or only a change in the nature of its constituent parts, is uncertain, and of no importance to determine" (XVI, 369). But that he is further concerned with the possible disintegration of his Mundane Universe is indicated by his constant return to the problem. For example, arguing against the possibility that Hell should have been created within the limits of the World, say, in the bowels of the earth, he says: "Besides, if, as has been shown from various passages of the New Testament, the whole world is to be consumed by fire, it follows that hell, being situated in the center of the earth, must share the fate of the surrounding universe, and perish likewise" (XVI, 375). In *Paradise Lost* Michael speaks of the time "When this world's dissolution shall be ripe"; God foretells that "The world shall burn" and be reduced to "ashes"; St. Francis, St. Dominic, and others must continue to wander in the Paradise of Fools "Till final dissolution," when no doubt the outer shell of the World shall crumble into its original chaotic elements. Moreover, God has extended his creative power into the visible World through his vicegerent, Nature, who has received both matter and forms from him and has combined them according to transmitted laws into varying degrees of perfection. In this creative process Chaos and Old Night are said to be her ancestors and chaos her womb, the eldest birth of which are the four elements. But now, having been instrumental in supervising creation of the World and in preserving its order according to laws handed down from God, she too must become involved in the final conflagration of her realm. When the World shall be dissolved, Nature's usefulness shall be ended. Then chaos shall become "perhaps her grave." It must be confessed, however, that this contingent "perhaps" would seem to reflect Milton's original uncertainty regarding whether the World shall be utterly dissolved into the substance of chaos or merely suffer changes in the nature and order of its constituent parts.

But after dissolution or alteration of the Mundane Universe, God's power goes forth again—still within the limits of space and vanishing time—in a final and ultimate creation, the creation of new heavens and a new earth. The origin of this new creation and the contour of its patterns are apocalyptic and can, therefore, be discerned only as through a glass darkly. It is not clear whether the new heaven and earth is, like the first heaven and earth, another instantaneous creation out of chaos materials or merely a renewal or renovation of the original World elements. In *The Christian Doctrine* Milton seems to support the latter view when he says: "Our glorification will be accompanied by the renovation of heaven and earth, and of all things therein" (XVI, 379). But in support of this conclusion he quotes from Revelation: "I saw a new heaven and a new earth; for the first heaven and the first earth were passed away; and there was no more sea: and I John saw the holy city, new Jerusalem, coming down from God out of Heaven, as a bride adorned for her husband" (XVI, 381). In *Paradise Lost* God says that from "ashes" of the burned World shall "spring" a new heaven and earth; but later he foresees that the old heaven and earth "renewed, shall be made pure." Michael is aware that temporal history shall continue to unfold "till fire purge all things new, / Both heaven and earth." But confused angels sing in praise of the Son "by whom / New Heaven and earth shall to the ages rise, / Or down from Heaven descend." By now it should be quite apparent that there is no definite solution of the problem as to whether this new heaven and earth shall descend like John's new Jerusalem from Heaven of Heavens or rise from the conflagrant mass of the World purged and refined. No cosmogonist is provided to explain the sources of primitive and crude materials employed—if any other than "ashes" of the burned World be needed. No physicist like Uriel appears to trace in detail the genesis of that Paradise on the new earth, where redeemed souls may choose to dwell rather than in the Heaven of Heavens. But it requires no ontologist to affirm the mystic truth that here as in all creations the essences of all things subsist "within" God who is Spirit and who is the only self-existent Being. The new Paradise is, therefore, a fitting home for his glorified saints. And in the apocalyptic suggestion of its eternally lighted grandeur the new creation may well serve as an addition to the original stage upon which Milton can properly represent the grand denouement of his profound drama in *Paradise Lost*.

Milton's Light Exhaling
from Darkness: A Study
in Symbols

WHEN IN PARADISE LOST MILTON SINGS OF LIGHT AND darkness he seems to involve himself in confusion, uncertainty, and contradiction. For example, at the beginning of Book III he hails Holy Light as the "offspring of heaven first-born," but we are left uncertain which was first-born, Light or Heaven. Presently, however, he asserts that Light existed "Before the heavens." Or, remembering that God is supposed to be Light, he surmises that perhaps Holy Light is "of the eternal coeternal beam," "Bright effluence of bright essence increate." Or if you prefer, says he, Light may be considered as a "pure ethereal stream, / Whose fountain who shall tell" (III, 1-10). At any rate, on the morning of the first day of creation "Darkness profound / Covered the abyss"; and when God said, "Let there be light," "forthwith light / Ethereal, first of things, quintessence pure / Sprung from the deep." At the end of this day the Celestial Choirs—themselves the "progeny of light" (V, 600)—did not forget to celebrate the occasion "when orient light / Exhaling first

from darkness they beheld; / Birthday of heaven and earth"
(VII, 243-245, 253-255). Likewise Adam, in his hymn to the
Creator, invoked the seven planets to "resound / His praise,
who out of darkness called up light" (V, 178-179). And the
climax of this congeries of cryptic statements is reached
when Milton records that Hell "As one great furnace flamed,
yet from those flames / No light, but rather darkness visible"
(I, 62-63). Though the Milton brotherhood may find no difficult problems here, the ordinary reader's perplexity is likely
to approach extreme bewilderment.

But in attempting to reduce Milton's philosophical observations to some sort of system, one need not suppose that
the poet is a mere eclectic juggling attractive fragments.
Any cosmogony must necessarily be extremely recondite.
Its vocabulary is, therefore, usually abstruse, mystic, and
symbolic. Milton, being tremendously interested in the ultimate origins and processes of creation, is apparently unwill-
ing to employ a private and personal symbology in the presentation of his concepts; he rather attaches himself to established traditions which furnish a terminology now become
reputable by virtue of long use. He discovers, however, that
the same traditional term is often used to symbolize several
stages in the process of creation or that a single stage may
be represented by a disturbing variety of symbols. But Milton is not confused: he has before him rabbinical commentaries upon the Torah,[1] the cabbalistic writings, and the
mystic speculations of the Neoplatonists.[2] These related
systems he has successfully syncretized and has gleaned
from them a wealth of symbols which he understands and
uses for poetic purposes. Let us assume with M. Saurat[3]
that he was thoroughly familiar with the *Zohar*, for example.
In that case, an investigation of the *Zohar* in comparison

with certain aspects of *Paradise Lost*—which is the purpose of the present study—may serve to clarify some of the poet's observations on light and darkness.

According to the *Zohar*, then, God the Ancient Holy One, Most Recondite, Limitless and therefore absolutely unknowable First Cause of all essences and movement, reveals himself as Creator of the universe in nine descending stages or degrees.[4] Three of these nonabsolute grades of the godhead are said to subsist on the Right, three on the Left, and three in the Center, though they are not conceived as being arranged in this consecutive order. But all stages of this graduated emanative series are considered to be concentrations of God's "thought" or "pools" of his creative power, all depending upon God, the First Grade.[5] In the present study we are concerned primarily with the second, third, fourth, and fifth stages of the creative process. And it must be remembered that these are all extremely hidden and mysterious manifestations, quite beyond the exoteric's apprehension or comprehension, belonging as they do to a realm wholly noumenal.

Initiated commentators in the *Zohar*, however, seem to be perfectly familiar with the origin, qualities, and symbolic powers of even the recondite Second Grade. It is identified with the cabbalistic *Hokmah*, Wisdom, and is called the Beginning, First Point, and Father.[6] Its creative energies are symbolized under the general term, *Light*. As to its origin the *Zohar* is explicit:

At the outset the decision of the King made a tracing in the supernal effulgence, a lamp of scintillation [respectively "darkness," "measurement"], and there issued within the impenetrable recesses of the mysterious limitless a shapeless nucleus [respectively "vapour"] enclosed in a ring, neither white nor black nor red nor green nor any colour at all. When he took measurements, he fashioned colours to show within, and within the lamp there issued a certain effluence from which colours were imprinted below. The most mysterious Power enshrouded in the limitless clave, as it were, without cleaving its void, remaining wholly unknowable until from the force of the strokes there shone forth a supernal and mysterious point. Beyond this point there is no knowable, and therefore it is called *Reshith* (beginning), the creative utterance which is the starting-point of all (I, 63, 15a).

Or in terms of the Light-symbol: "This word, *awr* (light), contains within itself a hidden significance. The expansive force proceeding from the hidden recesses of the secret supernal ether opened a path and produced from itself a mysterious point (or, rather, the *En Sof* (limitless) clave its own ether and disclosed this point), *Yod*. When this expanded, that which was left of the mysterious *AWIR* (ether) was found to be *AWR* (light) . . . and thus was light (*awr*) left from ether (*awir*). . . . This dot of the word *Awr* is Light (I, 69-70, 16b)." This primordial supernal First Point, this ethereal "veiled one," contains within itself in *potentia* the "sum of all existence" (I, 5); it is identified with that mysterious creator, *Mi* (who)—in the passage *Who created these?*—called "the extremity of Heaven on high" and "the extremity of Heaven above" (I, 4-5). This is the Lower Eden, the Ancient One, the architect of the universe.

Now the emanation of creative energy from the First Point into succeeding grades is presented in a variety of striking symbols. For example, the supernal point expands or extends itself, clothing itself in a luminous garment like a membrane for the brain (I, 84, 19b) or "just as the silkworm encloses itself, as it were, in a palace of its own production which is both useful and beautiful" (I, 63, 15a). Or a river flows out of Eden to water the Garden (IV, 215, 210b). Or Wisdom shapes the Crowns of all other emanations (IV, 109, 175b), or the Supernal Tree of Life kindles all of their lights (IV, 388, 34a). Or, as R. Simeon reports a tradition,

Out of this unknowable [Beginning] issued a slender thread of light which was itself concealed and invisible, but which yet contained all other lights, and which received vibrations from That which does not vibrate and reflected light from That which diffused it not. This slender thread in turn gave birth to another light wherein to disport and conceal itself; and in this light were woven and fashioned six impressions which are not known save to that slender light when it goes in to hide itself and shine through that other light. The light which issues from the slender light is mighty and terrible, and it expands and becomes a world which illumines all succeeding worlds (III, 358-359, 126b).

Mindful of these august symbols, we may perhaps discern some inkling of Milton's sublime concept when he addresses "holy light, offspring of heaven first-born." We have already seen that Wisdom, the Beginning of all things, is the height of "heaven" above; in the process of emanative creation, therefore, it is this Heaven which is "first-born." And that Holy Light which is the "offspring of heaven" may be identified with the slender thread of Light, concealed and invisible, which contains all other lights as it issues from the unknowable First Point. Moreover, in order to clarify his meaning further the poet avails himself of another symbol of like import: "Or hearest thou rather pure ethereal stream, / Whose fountain who shall tell." Authors of the *Zohar* have already revealed how the Expansive Force proceeding from the recesses of the secret supernal Ether produced from itself a mysterious Point (or, rather, the Limitless clave its own

Ether and disclosed this Point), how when this expanded
what was left of the mysterious Ether was found to be Light,
and how this Light was thus left from Ether. And we have
observed that from this Ethereal First Point there flows a
mighty stream of creative energy. Milton cannot be wrong,
therefore, when he hails Holy Light as a "pure ethereal
stream." And remembering the extremely secret and hidden
quality of the Ethereal First Point—it is almost as unknowable as the Most Recondite himself—he is constrained to
close his apostrophe to the pure Ethereal Stream with the
perplexed question, "Whose fountain who shall tell?"

But let us return to the process of emanative creation. As
has been said, the Beginning or First Point extends or expands, and it thus creates for itself a "Palace" or "Building"
for its honor and glory. This Palace is *Binah* (Understanding), the Third Grade of the godhead called *Elohim Hayyim*
(Living God). This is that Garden watered by the stream
which flows from Eden (IV, 215, 210b); it is that mysterious
Mah (What), designated as "the extremity of Heaven below" (I, 5); it is in general called "Mother" and "Earth."
Its position is on the Left, and its creative energy is a light
"mighty and terrible" or a "black fire" called Darkness (I,
70, 16b; I, 117, 31a). In this Palace, it is said, Wisdom
"sowed a seed which was to generate for the benefit of the
universe" (I, 63); or, from within this Lamp (First Point)
"there issued a certain effluence from which colours were
imprinted below" (I, 63, 15a); or, as we have seen, the
"slender light" emanating from Wisdom "in turn gave birth
to another light" in which were woven and fashioned six
impressions, and this light, expanding, "becomes a world . . .
a hidden and unknown world in which dwell six myriads
of thousands of supernal powers" (III, 358, 126b). Thus

the creative energy of the Third Grade becomes somewhat differentiated: here there is recognizable an active principle called "heaven" and a passive principle called "earth," which may be "identified with the primordial elements of the terrestrial, the celestial, and the spiritual worlds."[7] Here the active principle, heaven, is represented as the "Voice" of the Living God (I, 112, 29a) which, working upon the primordial elements of earth, produces through a series of utterances or commands the succeeding "days" of creation (I, 69, 16b). In this manner the impregnated "Mother" (or Palace sown with seed) becomes the artificer of the universe. At the command of the "Voice" there issues from this primordial "Darkness" a stream of creative power which produces the first "day" of creation.

That is to say, on the "one day" or first day of creation the "Voice" of Elohim said, "Let there be Light." And straightway creative energy flowing out of primordial Darkness produced the Fourth Grade of the godhead, called *Hesid* (Kindness or Love). Its position is on the Right, and its creative energy is therefore called "Light." Thus the "light" of the Fourth Grade is exhaled from that "Darkness" which is the Third Grade (I, 70, 16b). "Afterwards the great deep arose in Darkness, and darkness covered all, until light emerged and cleft the darkness and came forth and shone, as it is written, 'He uncovereth deep things out of Darkness, and bringeth out to light the shadow of death' " (I, 116, 30b). But the production of this Fourth Grade Light was, as the *Zohar* reports it, an exceedingly complicated and perplexing process. We must understand that the Third Grade heaven and earth (active and passive principles) had been approaching each other for the creation of actual being, which was as yet in a state of becoming. As Simon explains

it, "The earth in this stage is said to have been of two qualities: (a) 'formless' (*tohu*), and (b) 'inchoate' (*bohu*). Correspondingly, the heaven was of two qualities: (a) 'darkness on the face of the deep' (*t'hom*, identified by the *Zohar*
with *tohu*), and (b) 'the spirit of God moving over the face
of the waters' (identified by the *Zohar* with *bohu*)."[8] Or as
the *Zohar* expresses it in detail:

There was snow in the midst of water, from the action of
which was produced a slime. Then a mighty fire beat upon it
and produced in it a refuse. So it was transformed and became
Tohu (chaos), the abode of slime, the nest of refuse, and also
Bohu (formlessness), the finer part which was sifted from the
Tohu and rested upon it. The word "darkness" in the text alludes
to this mighty fire. This darkness covered the *Tohu*, namely the
refuse, and was buoyed up by it. The "Spirit of God" is a holy
spirit that proceeded from *Elohim Hayyim* (living God), and
this was "hovering over the face of the waters." When this wind
blew, a certain film detached itself from the refuse, like the film
which remains on the top of boiling broth when the froth has
been skimmed off two or three times. When *Tohu* had thus been
sifted and purified, there issued from it a "great and strong
wind." . . . Similarly *Bohu* was sifted and purified, and there
issued from it an earthquake. . . . Then what we call "darkness"
was sifted and there was contained in it fire. . . . When what we
call "spirit" was sifted, there was contained in it a still, small
voice.

Tohu is a place which has no colour and no form. . . . *Bohu*,
on the other hand, has shape and form. . . . "Darkness" is a black
fire, strong in colour. There is a red fire, strong in visibility; a
yellow fire, strong in shape; and a white fire, the colour which
includes all. "Darkness" is the strongest of all fires, and this is
what took hold on *Tohu*. "Darkness" is a fire, but fire is not
darkness, save when it takes hold of *Tohu*. . . . Hence this fire
is called "darkness" because it rested upon *Tohu*, and took hold
of it; this is the inner meaning of the words, "and darkness on

the face of the abyss." "Spirit" is the voice which rests on *Bohu,* and grasps it and guides it as required. This is symbolized in the words, "The voice of the Lord was hovering on the waters"; and so, too, "the spirit of the Lord was hovering over the face of the waters" (I, 66-68, 16a).

Here symbololatry of the *Zohar* seems to have attained the height (or depth) of obscurity and complexity. But it is quite clear that it is the quality of Third Grade "heaven" (active principle) called the "Voice" or Spirit of the Lord, hovering over, grasping, and directing that quality of "earth" (passive principle) called *bohu,* which has produced that "Light" which is the Fourth Grade of the godhead.

This Light of the Fourth Grade is complex. According to Maurice Simon, it may itself be differentiated into a trilogy of "lights": one on the right called "light" (which was withdrawn as soon as it emerged, I, 120, 31b); one in the center called "firmament" (perhaps "light proper, which moved to the right, taking the place of that light which disappeared") and one on the left called "darkness" (which is the light of fire). " 'And God saw the light (i.e., the centre) that it was good, and God divided between the light (i.e., the right) from the darkness.' The centre was therefore given continued existence in a category of time called day, and the darkness in a category of time called night."[9] Or as R. Isaac of the *Zohar* explains the situation: "That radiance which God produced at the time of the Creation illumined the world from one end to the other, but was withdrawn. . . . This light issued from the darkness which was carved out by strokes of the Most Recondite; and similarly from that light which was stored away there was carved out through some hidden process the lower-world darkness in which light resides. This lower darkness is what is called 'night' in the verse, 'and darkness he called night' " (I, 120, 32a). Or as R. Simeon has it:

Light came forth on the right side and darkness on the left, and God afterwards separated them in order again to unite them, as it is written, "And God divided the light from the darkness." This does not mean that there was an absolute separation, but that the day came from the side of light, which is the right, and night from the side of darkness, which is the left, and that, having emerged together, they were separated in such a way as to be no longer side by side but face to face . . . the light being called day and the darkness night, as it says, "And God called the light day and the darkness he called night." This is the darkness that is attached to night, which has no light of its own, although it comes from the side of that primordial fire which is called "darkness" (I, 117, 31a).

The difference by means of which light is distinguished from darkness is one of degree only; both are one in kind, as there is no light without darkness and no darkness without light; but though one, they are different in colour (I, 121, 32a).

Moreover, differentiation of the Fourth Grade Light is represented by further symbolic and occult terminology. For example, that "light" which exists in the category of time called day is said to be "male," and darkness or night on the left is "female" (I, 121, 32a); or the right is "heaven" and the left is "earth"; or the male may be identified with "upper waters" and the female with "lower waters," though the former yet holds the latter in solution, as it were. We have already seen how in the Upper World (i.e., the first three Grades of the godhead) Wisdom is in general called "Heaven" and Understanding "Earth," but how in Understanding "heaven" and "earth" (active and passive principles) become differentiated for the first time. So also in each of the six lower Grades (i.e., in the Lower World) there may be discerned a "heaven" and "earth" according to the supernal pattern. As the *Zohar* says:

In this way the so-called supernal *Elohim* made a heaven and earth for permanency, and produced them together by the supernal energy, the starting point of all. The supernal essence then descended to a lower grade, and this latter made a heaven and earth below. . . . There are two Worlds and they created worlds, one an upper world and one a lower world, one corresponding to the other; one created heaven and earth and the other created heaven and earth. . . .

When the upper world was filled and became pregnant, it brought forth two children together, male and female, these being heaven and earth after the supernal pattern. The earth is fed from the waters of heaven which are poured into it. These upper waters, however, are male, whereas the lower waters are female, and the lower are fed from the male and the lower waters call to the upper, like a female that receives the male, and pour out water to meet the water of the male to produce seed (I, 113, 29b).

But it must be understood that on this first day of creation the upper and lower waters were not yet divided, that "all the powers of the earth were latent and not productive, and the waters were frozen in it" (I, 116, 30b) until the Voice said, "Let there be Light." These waters "only spread abroad when light from above was shed upon the earth" (*ibid.*).

If these speculations of the *Zohar* have any validity in them, then Milton is correct when he says that Holy Light, offspring of Heaven the first-born, existed "before the heavens" of all succeeding grades. He also understands how, in preparation for the first day of creation, "the great deep arose in Darkness, and darkness covered all, until light emerged and cleft the darkness and came forth and shone," and how, at the Voice of God, one element of Fourth Grade

Light invested "as with a mantle . . . / The rising world of waters dark and deep" (*PL.*, III, 10-11). He knows that this "Light" is ultimately "Ethereal, first of things" and that on this first day it "Sprung from the deep." No one need be surprised, therefore, if the Celestial Choirs celebrate the day "when orient light / Exhaling first from darkness they beheld; / Birthday of [Fourth Grade] heaven and earth." Adam also shows himself esoteric when he calls upon the spheres to "resound / His praise who out of darkness called up light." And whenever the Angels were created, they must necessarily be, like everything else in the universe, the "progeny" of that original, most recondite Holy Light.

Now on the second day of creation a conflict arose. This is the Fifth Grade of the godhead, called *Geburah* (Force), and its position is unfortunately on "the Left." Here an expansive force called "Firmament" (content of the second day and, therefore, different from the firmament of the first day) separated "upper waters" from "lower waters" or differentiated "male" from "female" (I, 72, 17a).[10] This Firmament was produced by that quality of Third Grade "heaven" (active principle) called Darkness or "black fire" which took hold upon that quality of "earth" (passive principle) called *tohu*—"darkness on the face of the abyss"; and being situated on "the Left," its luminosity was "dark" in comparison with the Light of the first day. The *Zohar* offers no specific explanation as to why conflict arose between the first and second days of creation; it merely states that creation on the second day was "defective" and incomplete. "Here discord was created through that which is called 'the Left.' . . . When the Left awoke, there awoke discord, and through that discord the wrathful fire was reinforced and there emerged from it Gehinnom, which originated from the left and continued there" (I, 72, 17a). Or as R. Isaac has it: "On the second day was created Gehinnom for sinners; on the second day, too, was created conflict. On the second day the work begun was not finished, and therefore the words 'and it was good' are not used in connection with it" (I, 144, 46a). Or in similar vein it is reported that:

In the work of creation there was an antagonism of the left against the right, and the division between them allowed the Gehinnom to emerge and to fasten itself on the left. Then the Central Column, which is the third day, intervened and allayed the discord between the two sides, so that the Gehinnom descended below. . . . It was on the second that, before the discord was allayed, the Gehinnom was created. Then also were created all the angels who revolted against their Master, and whom the fire of Gehinnom consumed and destroyed; likewise all those others who vanish away and do not endure and are consumed by fire (I, 72-74, 17a).

Here we are concerned especially with the origin and characteristics of Gehinnom in terms of the light-symbol. It must be recalled that when the primordial Darkness of the Third Grade was sifted, there was contained in it fire—a black fire, the strongest and mightiest of all fires. This fire of Darkness took hold upon *Tohu* (Chaos) and was buoyed up by it; that is to say, "Darkness was upon the face of the abyss." And it was the action of this black fire or Darkness upon *Tohu* (Chaos or refuse) which produced on the Left that "darkness" which is identical with the Firmament of the second day of creation. Thus Light of the first day was brought into conflict with darkness of the second day; Right was arrayed against Left. Meanwhile darkness (the Left) flamed forth with a most vehement fire; "when darkness asserted itself, it did so with fury, and created Gehinnom"

(I, 73, 17b). Now in order to understand the process by which Gehinnom was produced, it is necessary to observe that normally darkness desired to merge itself in Light (i.e., the Left in the Right), but the furious conflict between them prevented this consummation for a time. Darkness was "not strong enough to merge itself in the Right"; as a consequence, during the conflict "night" spread from it. But when "night" began to spread, and before it was complete, what remained of darkness went and merged itself in the Right, and thus "night" was left defective. In this manner "darkness abated its light," and there was produced a grade which was defective and not radiant. This defective, nonradiant element of flaming darkness is Gehinnom. And since its "night" or detached portion of darkness can never be merged in the Right, its flames are forever without light; as the *Zohar* concludes, "Darkness does not radiate save when it is merged in Light" (I, 71, 17a). In this manner the origin and qualities of Gehinnom are revealed. And through the symbolism employed—if the rabbinical Gehinnom may be identified in some sense with Christian Hell—one can discern a possible similar meaning in Milton's description of the abode of Satan and his fallen angels: "A dungeon horrible, on all sides round / As one great furnace flamed, yet from those flames / No light, but rather darkness visible" (*PL.*, I, 61-63).

It does not seem necessary here to investigate the process of creation through the last four grades of revealed godhead. But it is well to observe that Milton ventures hesitantly—he hopes without blame—to peer into the incomprehensible sanctity of God's privity. Zoroaster,[11] St. John,[12] and others[13] have furnished him with the sublime symbol, "God is Light"; and St. Paul has conceived of the "only Potentate, the King of Kings" as "dwelling in the light which no man can approach unto; whom no man hath seen, nor can see."[14] He perhaps remembers that Hermes Trismegistus saw a "light, a joyous light" and heard Poimandres, the mind of Sovereignty, say, "That Light is I, even Mind, the first God."[15] He is aware that the First Point was a tracing in the "supernal effulgence" and that it "reflected light from That which diffused it not." Or like the cabbalists, he may imagine that God is, as it were, an Eternal and Absolute Light sending forth its beams in all directions and that these rays are reflected, as in a glass, from each succeeding manifestation to the next.[16] And being unable to conceive of this Eternal Light apart from its radiating rays, the poet (or philosopher) is moved to speak of Holy Light as "of the eternal coeternal beam." In addition, wishing to maintain and emphasize the distinction between creation as a separate product of God's activity and creation as emanation of undiminished divine power, he hails Light as "Bright effluence of bright essence increate."

Thus in Milton's speculations regarding light and darkness—their origin, qualities, and relationship—there is apparently discoverable neither confusion nor contradiction. There is merely a shifting of the Light-symbol from one secondary Grade to another and finally to the Most Recondite himself. And recognition of a further shifting is inevitable when we consider that there is a precise correspondence between the invisible and the visible worlds, that the ten Grades of the godhead discussed above are noumenal, serving as a sort of pattern for the phenomenal, or that the phenomenal is a reflection of the noumenal. It is therefore fitting that, in representing the six days' production of the visible cosmos, the poet should employ symbols applicable in the creation of the invisible world. Here also on the first day God said, "Let there be Light," and straightway visible Light—still the active principle of creative energy—"Sprung from the deep, and from her native east[17] / To journey through the airy gloom began." And on the fourth day a large portion of this same creative, lifegiving energy was poured into the body of the Sun, which henceforth became the source of all light and life in the visible universe.

NOTES

CHAPTER ONE

[1] *De Doctrina Christiana*, ed., with trans. of Charles R. Sumner, by James Holly Hanford and Waldo Hilary Dunn, in *The Works of John Milton*, gen. ed., Frank Allen Patterson (18 vols. in 21, New York, 1931-1938), XIV-XVII. Parenthetical references in the text are to this edition.

[2] See *Plotini Opera Omnia*, ed. Fridericus Creuzer (3 vols., Oxford, 1835); *Plotinos; Complete Works*, trans. Kenneth Sylvan Guthrie (4 vols. in 1, 2nd ed., London, 1918), *Ennead*, VI.v.1; Porphyry, *Commentaries or Outlines of the Enneads of Plotinos, ibid.*, 1226; Cicero, *De Natura Deorum*, ed. and trans. H. Rackham, Loeb Classical Library (London, 1933), I.i, and *Tusculan Disputations*, ed. and trans. J. E. King, Loeb Classical Library (London, 1927), I.xvi.

[3] Richard McKeon, (ed. and trans.), *Selections from Medieval Philosophers* (2 vols., New York, 1929-1930), II, 453.

[4] *Summa Theologica*, trans. Fathers of the English Dominican Province (22 vols., London, 1912-1925), I.29.2 *ad* 3.

[5] *Metaphysics*, ed. and trans. Hugh Tredennick, Loeb Classical Library (2 vols., London, 1933-1935), X.i.8.

[6] *Sum. Theol.*, I.xi.3c.

[7] *The True Intellectual System of the Universe* (2 vols., 1st Am. ed., Andover, 1837), I, 282.

[8] *Metaphysics*, XII.vii.12-13.

[9] See William Ralph Inge, *The Philosophy of Plotinus* (2 vols., 3d ed., New York, 1929), II, 107-109.

[10] For a full discussion of this concept, see G. L. Prestige, *God in Patristic Thought* (London, 1936), *passim*, and especially 197 ff. Cf. Frank Egleston Robbins, *The Hexaemeral Literature* (Chicago, 1912), 52, 71, 74.

[11] *Metaphysics*, V.viii.4. Cf. XII.iii.3-4.

[12] *Sum. Theol.*, I.29.2c. For meaning of terms, see McKeon, II, 500 ff.

[13] McKeon, II, 500.

[14] See Prestige, 228.

[15] In Milton's system, the Son cannot be identified with *Hokmah* or Wisdom of the Cabbalistic philosophy, because the latter as first emanation contains within itself all possible further developments. See Christian D. Ginsburg, *The Kabbalah* (London, 1925), 138 ff.; *The Zohar*, trans. H. Sperling and M. Simon (5 vols., London, 1931-1934), I, 385. On Wisdom, see Harris Francis Fletcher's stimulating *Milton's Rabbinical Readings* (Urbana, 1930), 116 ff.

[16] See *infra*, 60-63.

[17] *Metaphysics*, XII.vi.3-4.

[18] *Sum. Theol.*, I.ii.3; I.iii.2c.

[19] This is a scholastic term which Sumner mistranslates "essentially" somewhat contrary to Milton's meaning. See McKeon's definition: *"eminently;* a thing is contained eminently in something else more excellently than in itself . . . as the perfection of effects . . . found in analogical or equivocal causes . . . ; in this analogical sense the perfections of creatures are to be found in God, and God is the eminent cause of things" (II, 450).

[20] This idea is of ancient origin. See, for example, *Hermetica*, ed. and trans. Walter Scott (4 vols., Oxford, 1924-1936), Libellvs XI.ii.18, and Scott's commentary II, 325; Cudworth, I, 409-412, where he quotes from Neoplatonists, Orphic philosophers, and others.

[21] I have traced the concept of matter's goodness to Proclus, *infra*, 61.

[22] See *infra*, 169.

[23] *A Fuller Institution of the Art of Logic*, ed. and trans. Allan H. Gilbert, in *Works*, XI, 53.

[24] *Ibid.*, 51.

[25] *De Generatione et Corruptione*, trans. Harold H. Joachim (Oxford, 1922), 333b.25-30; cf. *Sum. Theol.*, I.lxvi.2c.

[26] On the emanation of space, see *infra*, 53-54.

[27] *Sum. Theol.*, I.liii.1c.

[28] *Ibid.*, I.xviii.1c; I.xviii.4 *ad* 1.

[29] *Ibid.*, I.lxvi.4 *ad* 3.

[30] *Ibid.*, I.lxvi.1c.

[31] *Ibid.;* cf. Robbins, 46, 67.

[32] "Of the Existence and Nature of God," in *Select Discourses* (2d ed., Cambridge, 1673), 140.

[33] *Ibid.* For further illustration of God as distributor of life and energy, see *Hermetica*, Libellvs XI.1-2; Libellvs II.6a; Asclepius III.29c, and Scott's notes to same.

[34] See *infra*, 105-106, and my *Shakespeare's Philosophical Patterns* (Baton Rouge, 1937), 32 ff.; Robbins, 15 ff., 68 ff.

[35] *Select Discourses*, 140-141.

[36] *Commentaries*, in *Plotinos; Complete Works*, 1241.

[37] *Ibid.*, 1240.

[38] *On the Confusion of Tongues*, XXVII.134-136, ed. and trans. F. H. Colson and G. H. Whitaker (10 vols., London, 1929-1941), IV, 83.

39 *Enneads* VI.v.4, in *Complete Works*, 318.

40 *Commentaries,* in *Plotinos; Complete Works*, 1244.

41 *Ibid.,* 1249.

42 Cudworth, II, 204-207, presents in great detail this matter supported by copious extracts from Greek texts.

43 See Maurice Kelley's illuminating work, *This Great Argument* (Princeton, 1941), *passim.*

44 *Paradise Lost,* ed. Harris Francis Fletcher, in *The Complete Poetical Works of John Milton* (Boston, 1941). In the text, references in parentheses are to this edition.

45 For somewhat different interpretations of the passage, VII, 168-173, see Kelley, 82, and George Coffin Taylor, *Milton's Use of Du Bartas* (Cambridge, Mass., 1934), 42. In the light of Milton's clearly expressed dual concept of God, Denis Saurat's "retraction" theory seems contradictory, irrational, and naive; see *Milton: Man and Thinker* (New York, 1925), 123-125.

46 See, for example, my *Shakespeare's Philosophical Patterns*, 174 ff., and "Destiny in Chaucer's *Troilus,*" *PMLA*, XLV (1930), 129-134, for such representation of Fate or Destiny by Proclus, Iamblichus, Boethius, and Olympiodorus.

47 Cf. Ben Gray Lumpkin's excellent study, "Fate in *Paradise Lost,*" *SP*, XLIV (1947), 56-68.

48 Most of the symbols in this diagram are universally accepted in Christian tradition, but the ordering of them is in strict accord with Milton's peculiar concepts. Here one may recognize the unknowable Jehovah in the tetragrammaton (JHVH); God conceived as Creator on his Mount in Heaven of Heavens, clothed in Light and radiating infinite Light; Christ the Son of God represented in the *chi-rho, alpha* and *omega* symbol, and Jesus, the incarnate Christ, represented by the cross; and the Holy Spirit appearing in the usual symbol, a dove. All "external" creations, Heaven of Heavens, Hell, chaos, and the Cosmos (with all their contents) are still found to be "within" an incomplete triangle, symbolizing the Trinity. This triangle is incomplete at the apex, thus symbolizing Milton's unwillingness to accept the orthodox concept of the Trinity. The symbol for Christ and the symbol for the Holy Spirit are much smaller than that for Jehovah, therefore, and are placed within the shadow of the JHVH. The flaming nimbus in circular form symbolizes Eternity, or the effluence of the Divine Essence through all Eternity.

49 The substance of this chapter appeared first in *Studies in Philology,* XLVII (1950), 190-210.

CHAPTER TWO

1 Milton offers meager information about these divinities; for further references, see *Paradise Lost,* I, 543; II, 133, 894 ff., 907 ff., 964 ff., 968 ff.; III, 18; VI, 871; X, 83, 477 ff.

[2] Marjorie Nicolson, "Milton and the *Conjectura Cabbalistica*," *Philological Quarterly*, VI (1927), 12.

[3] C. G. Osgood, *The Classical Mythology of Milton's English Poems* (New York, 1900), 22. Cf. Francis Bacon: "Now, as touching chaos, that by the ancients was never dignified with divine honor, or with the title of a god." *The Wisdom of the Ancients*, 17, in *The Works of Francis Bacon*, ed. Basil Montagu (3 vols., Philadelphia, 1852), I, 298.

[4] Osgood, xviii-xix. Cf. Newton's remark: "All the ancient naturalists, philosophers, and poets held that *Chaos* was the first principle of all things; and the poets particularly make *Night* a goddess, and represent *Night* or darkness, and *Chaos* or confusion, as exercising uncontrolled dominion from the beginning." Quoted from A. W. Verity, *Paradise Lost* (Cambridge, England, 1921), 423. "But," continues Verity, "in personifying Chaos as a distinct divinity Milton seems to have extended the classical conception." Cf. Thomas Hobbes: "The uniform matter of the world was a God, by the name of *Chaos*." *Leviathan*, ed. A. R. Waller (Cambridge, England, 1904), 74.

[5] Osgood, xviii-xix. Cf. Verity, 423.

[6] *The Mystical Hymns of Orpheus*, trans, Thomas Taylor (London, 1896), 10.

[7] *The Six Books of Proclus on the Theology of Plato*, trans. Thomas Taylor (2 vols., London, 1816), I, 158-166.

[8] *Ibid.*, 177-222 *(intelligible triads)*; 223-309 *(intelligible and at the same time intellectual orders)*; 310-425 *(intellectual)*; II, 3-54 *(supermundane)*; II, 57-89 *(liberated)*; II, 90-122 *(mundane)*. See also Taylor, Additional Notes, *ibid.*, II, xix.

[9] *Ibid.*, II, xiv. The relationships between members of this triad are so complex that the discerning eye may recognize in each a further triple division. But we shall make little or no use of the concept of a triad of triads.

[10] *Ibid.*, I, 167.

[11] *Ibid.*, 173.

[12] *Ibid.*, 169-173, *passim*.

[13] *Ibid.*, 173.

[14] *Ibid.*, 182.

[15] *Ibid.*, 232-261, *passim*.

[16] *Ibid.*, 244.

[17] *Ibid.*, 245. Cf. also I, 88-89.

[18] Damascius, *Concerning Principles*, trans. Thomas Taylor, *ibid.*, Additional Notes, II, xv.

[19] *Ibid.*, xvi.

[20] See *The Mystical Hymns of Orpheus*, 18-20, for the hymn *To Protogonus* and Taylor's interpretation.

[21] *The Six Books of Proclus*, II, xvi.

[22] *On the Cratylus of Plato*, *ibid.*, Additional Notes, II, xxv.

[23] *Ibid.*, xxv, n. 1.

24 See *The Mystical Hymns of Orpheus*, 10-11, where Taylor emphasizes such identification.

25 Reported by Damascius, II, xvii.

26 *Ibid.*

27 *Ibid.* So Epimenides, *ibid.*

28 *Ibid.*

29 Hesiod, *Theogony*, ed. and trans. Hugh G. Evelyn-White for Loeb Classical Library (London, 1926), 87, lines 116-125.

30 *The Mystical Hymns of Orpheus*, XV, *To Jupiter*, 46. See Taylor's explanation of the hymn in terms of Neoplatonic theology, *ibid.*, 46, n. 43.

31 See Ralph Cudworth, *The True Intellectual System of the Universe*, I, 404, where he supports this thesis by quotations from Orphic theology and the Christian bishop Synesius. This notion of a bisexual deity is probably of Egyptian origin; see *The Poimandres* of Hermes Trismegistus, ed. and trans. Walter Scott, in *Hermetica*, Libellvs I.9 (I, 119), where the first Mind is said to be "bisexual," and *Asclepius*, III.20b (I, 333) where he is represented as being "filled with all fecundity of both sexes in one." Scott (III, 135-136) gives many parallels to this idea in ancient Egyptian documents; it is also to be found widespread in the religions of Asia Minor (III, 125, n. 1), in the Orphic Theogonia (III, 126), in the Gnostic writings (III, 136), and elsewhere. Denis Saurat, *Milton: Man and Thinker*, 291-292, probably lays too much stress on the *Zohar* as the source for Milton's treatment of this "delicate" subject.

32 *The Mystical Hymns of Orpheus*, 48; Cudworth, I, 404.

33 On the analogous subsistence of these two principles, male and female, in all orders, see *The Six Books of Proclus*, II, 191-192.

34 *The Mystical Hymns of Orpheus*, III, *To Night*, 10.

35 See Damascius, Additional Notes, II, xviii; Cudworth (quoting Damascius), I, 450.

36 Damascius, II, xvii; *Hermetica*, II, 126.

37 *The Poimandres* of Hermes Trismegistus, in *Hermetica*, Libellvs I.4 (I, 115). Cf. Libellvs III.1b.

38 *A Fuller Institution of the Art of Logic*, in *Works*, XI, 59.

39 *The Six Books of Proclus*, I, 173. On the mysterious manner in which intelligible essence comes into subsistence from the superessential *bound* and *infinity*, see *ibid.*, 172 ff.

40 Cf. W. Windelband, *A History of Philosophy*, trans. James H. Tufts (New York, 1931), 251.

41 Proclus, *On the Nature of Evil*, trans. Kenneth Sylvan Guthrie, 34, in *Proclus's Life, Hymns & Works* (North Yonkers, New York, 1925).

42 *Ibid.*, 39.

43 *Ibid.*, 38.

44 *Ibid.*, 46. Proclus initiates here the concept that matter was originally good, or at least not evil. Plotinus had maintained that matter is Negation or Non-Being and therefore Evil itself. *Enneads*, I.vm.3, in *Plotini Opera*

Omnia. Milton is evidently following Proclus, or his successors, when he derives matter from God and concludes: "For the original matter of which we speak, is not to be looked upon as an evil or trivial thing, but as intrinsically good, and the chief productive stock of every subsequent good." *De Doctrina Christiana,* XV, 23.

[45] Proclus, *On Evil,* 33.

[46] *Ibid.*

[47] See Plotinus, for example, *Enneads,* I.viii.4; IV.iii.9.

[48] Robert Fludd expresses a similar conception: "Unde mundi mater vocatur, in cujus gremio . . . quatuor elementa inferius juxta centrum suspensa tanquam in utero materno comprehenduntur. Hujus autem materiae informis effigiem imaginariam, *Mercurii Trismegisti* & veridici *Moysis* discriptionem imitando, sub forma *fumi nigerrimi,* seu vaporis, seu umbrae horrendae . . . depinximus." *Utrisque Cosmi Maioris scilicet et Minoris Metaphysica, Physica atque Technica Historia* (2 vols., Oppenheim, 1617), I, 25. Cf. Avencebrol, *Fons Vitae,* ed. Clemens Baeumker (Münster, 1895), IV.18.

[49] Proclus, *On Evil,* 42.

[50] See Plato, *Timaeus,* ed. and trans. R. G. Bury, Loeb Classical Library (London, 1929), 52D-53B. We must observe here that, for Milton and the English Platonists of the seventeenth century, such theories of emanation as that of Proclus—involving a timeless, necessary, and eternal process—did not conflict with the conception of a historical creation consummated by an act of divine will. Having derived matter and chaos from God by the emanative process, Milton proceeds to represent the ordering of a part of chaos—as if it were the *first* composite body—into the cosmos by a special volitional act of God. But we are not concerned in this study with the creation of the World out of chaos in time.

[51] *On Evil,* 43.

[52] *Ibid.* Milton is, therefore, perfectly accurate when he speaks of "The rising world of waters dark and deep / Won from the void and formless infinite" (*PL.,* III, 11-12).

[53] *On Evil,* 38. Fludd, I, 25, while agreeing with Plato on the infinite capacity of prime matter for receiving forms, is doubtful about its infinity of extension, "nam Deus tantum scit, quam late sese haec potentia ultra mundi convexitatem extendat."

[54] Cf. Fludd, I, 26, on darkness as privation of light. Milton, *Paradise Regained,* in *Complete Poetical Works,* IV, 397-400, speaks of natural darkness as being "Privation mere of light." But concerning the original darkness out of which God caused the light to shine, he says, "That this darkness was far from being a mere negation, is clear," *De Doctrina Christiana,* XV, 17. It should also now be clear why Milton speaks (*PL.,* II, 438-440) of "the void profound / Of unessential night / . . . wide-gaping"; since the essences transmitted by Night into chaos are nothing but vestiges, he may describe her here as being unessential, i.e., void of true essences.

55 The poet here calls Night "uncreated" because she is disordered, unadorned, illogical, undigested, and without figure; *to create* means to order, reduce to measure, to digest. See *De Doctrina Christiana*, XV, 23. The phrase, "devoid of sense and motion" (*PL.*, II, 151), does not refer to Night, as some commentators have thought; it describes rather the possible final state of rebellious angels as conceived by Belial.

56 Cudworth indeed lumps Chaos and Night together as "senseless matter blindly and fortuitously moved." I, 344.

57 Diogenes Laertius, *Lives of Eminent Philosophers*, trans. R. D. Hicks, Loeb Classical Library (London, 1925), VIII.25. Cf. *Hermetica*, III, 22, for Numenius' report of a like Pythagorean opinion, and *Asclepius*, I.3c for apparent agreement. Scott, *ibid.*, also says that "Eudorus, a syncretic Platonist of Alexandria in the time of Augustus, held that *hyle* is derived from 'the One,' i.e., from God."

58 This is Porphyry's interpretation. Cudworth, I, 495.

59 *Ibid.*, 494.

60 Iamblichus, *On the Mysteries of the Egyptians, Chaldeans, and Assyrians*, trans. Thomas Taylor (London, 1895), VIII.III.303-304. Cf. *De mysteriis Aegyptiorum, Chaldaeorum, Assyriorum*, trans. Marsilius Ficinus (Venice, 1516), 20: "Materiam uero produxit deus materialitate, uidelicet ab essentialitate subderiuata"; or, as Cudworth, I, 450, reproduces the phrasing of Scutellius, "ab essentialitate succissa ac subscissa materialitate."

61 Quoted from Cudworth, I, 393.

62 *Ibid.*, 403.

63 *Select Passages Illustrating Neoplatonism*, trans. E. R. Dodds (London, 1923), 98; Proclus elsewhere calls matter "a child of God," *ibid.*, 98 n. See also *On Evil*, 43; *The Six Books of Proclus*, Additional Notes, II, xx; Cudworth, I, 450.

64 Cudworth, I, 394, 450.

65 *The Six Books of Proclus*, Additional Notes, II, xx.

66 *On Evil*, 41.

67 Cudworth, I, 450.

68 Proclus, *On Evil*, 64.

69 The substance of this chapter appeared first in *The Journal of English and Germanic Philology*, XLVI (1947), 38-52.

CHAPTER THREE

1 Aristotle, of course, recognized hot, cold, moist and dry as primary qualities. But it is doubtful whether anybody before Locke distinguished clearly between primary and secondary qualities. Milton, however, includes the qualities falling under both designations in his presentation of chaos.

2 See *supra*, 36-37.

3 *Ibid.*, 60-63.

⁴ On the popularity of atomism in seventeenth-century philosophy and literature, see Charles T. Harrison, "Bacon, Hobbes, Boyle, and the Ancient Atomists," *Harvard Studies and Notes in Philology and Literature*, XV (1933), 191-218, and "The Ancient Atomists and English Literature of the Seventeenth Century," *Harvard Studies in Classical Philology*, XLV (1934), 1-79; J. A. Comenius, *Naturall Philosophie Reformed by Divine Light or A Synopsis of Physicks* (London, 1650), 28 ff. Katherine Brownell Collier, *Cosmogonies of Our Fathers* (New York, 1934), 339: in the seventeenth century "Matter was generally conceived to be a chaos of particles."

⁵ On Democritus, see Aristotle, *De Caelo*, trans. J. L. Stocks (Oxford, 1922), 275b.20; 303a.10; 300.B9; 33a.5; *De Generatione et Corruptione*, 314a.21-24; 315b.6-15, etc.; Theodor Gomperz, *Greek Thinkers*, trans. Laurie Magnus (4 vols., London, 1912-1920), I, 316-369; Windelband, *A History of Philosophy*, 109-116, etc.; Cyril Bailey, *The Greek Atomists and Epicurus* (Oxford, 1928), 109-124.

⁶ Gomperz, I, 334.

⁷ *Ibid.*, 337.

⁸ *Ibid.*, 335.

⁹ Quoted in Harrison, *Harvard Studies and Notes in Philology and Literature*, XV (1933), 218 ff.

¹⁰ *Epicurus, The Extant Remains*, trans. Cyril Bailey (Oxford, 1926), *To Herodotus*, 23-25, 31-37; Lucretius, *On the Nature of Things*, trans. Thomas Jackson (Oxford, 1929), 11-45. Milton has no use for the uniformity of motion attributed by Epicurus to all atoms, whether single or in combination, nor for the Lucretian doctrine of the "swerve" of down-falling particles.

¹¹ Reported by Aristotle with some perplexity, *De Caelo*, 303a.5-25.

¹² *Ibid.*, 302a.11; 277b.14; 298b.8.

¹³ *De Gen. et Cor.*, 331b.

¹⁴ Lucretius, I.797-803. Cf. II.1112 f.

¹⁵ See *A Fuller Institution of the Art of Logic*, in *Works*, XI: "In the order of nature matter follows the efficient cause, and is a sort of effect of the efficient cause; for the efficient cause prepares the matter that it may be fit for receiving the form. As the efficient cause is that which first moves, so the matter is that which is first moved" (51). "Matter is commonly divided into primary and secondary; the secondary into proximate and remote" (53). I have further discussed this question, *infra*, 166.

¹⁶ See *infra*, 104-105, for a clarification of the terms *waters* (X, 285) and *fluid mass* (VII, 237) as applied to any portion of undigested chaotic matter. Comenius (28) identifies Moses' "waters" and "darkness" with "a vapour or a fume . . . a Chaos of dispersed Atomes, cohering in no part thereof." I have defined Raphael's *fluid mass* as "a sort of compound containing in solution or *in potentia* all possible elements and material aspects of the visible Universe."

¹⁷ Quoted in Verity, *Milton, Paradise Lost*, 597.

18 *Infra*, Chapter 6.

19 Evil angels would seem able actually to manipulate some aspects of the chaos-consistence. It is clear that the foundation of created Heaven of Heavens consists of several layers or grades of materials extending downward from the ethereal floor to chaos, upon which Heaven rests. Followers of Satan dig through the ethereous mold of the Heavenly landscape until they discover hidden veins of mineral and stone—not unlike those found in Earth's entrails; these are "The originals of nature in their crude / Conception" (VI, 510 ff.). Further down they search for "materials dark and crude, / Of spiritous and fiery spume" which, says Satan, "in their dark nativity the deep / Shall yield us, pregnant with infernal flame" (VI, 478 f.). From this passage one might reasonably conclude that, in the subtle art of making explosives, Satan's followers reveal power to command the potentials of primitive chaos.

20 For a full discussion of this conception, see *infra*, 107-109.

21 See *infra*, 150.

22 Cf. Verity's note, 409.

23 *Paradise Regained*, IV, 400.

24 Gomperz, I, 333.

25 See St. Augustine, *Against the Epistle of Manichaeus Called Fundamental*, chaps. 15, 20, 21, 24, trans. Richard Stothert, *Nicene and Post-Nicene Fathers* (Buffalo, 1887), IV, with Introduction by Albert H. Newman, 11-12.

26 See *supra*, 64.

27 Even allegorical and symbolical figures engage in clamorous uproar, "feel" tenfold confusion, and "hear" "unsufferable noise" (II, 967; III, 709; VI, 871; X, 478.

28 Taylor, *Milton's Use of Du Bartas*.

29 Du Bartas, *His Divine Weekes and Workes*, trans. Josvah Sylvester (London, 1621), 6.

30 *The Poimandres* of Hermes Trismegistus, in *Hermetica*, Libellvs I.4-5a.

31 For a detailed account of the relation between "first things" and "last things" in the Judaeo-Christian traditions, see Hermann Gunkel, *Schöpfung und Chaos in Urzeit und Endzeit* (Göttingen, 1895), *passim*, but especially 99-111.

32 See *infra*, 144-146.

33 *Epicurus, The Extant Remains*, 35 ff.

34 This is Cyril Bailey's commentary on *ibid.*, 213-214.

35 The allegorical "individuals," Sin and Death, are represented as emerging upward from Hellmouth; they fly "diverse" through chaos and meet "solid" or slimy materials which seem to them to be "as in raging sea / Tossed up and down" (X, 286-287).

36 Verity, 423.

37 The substance of this chapter appeared first in *Vanderbilt Studies in the Humanities*, I (1951), 56-70.

CHAPTER FOUR

[1] See *supra,* Chapter 3.

[2] See *infra,* 162, 99-100: "Here it is necessary to understand that Milton is not following that tradition which conceives of ether as a fifth essence differing in kind from all the four elements. He holds rather to the historical theory that ether is a matter sublimated from the four elements, or merely a purer form of air and fire."

[3] The Epicurean "To Pythocles," in *Epicurus, The Extant Remains,* no. 88, 6-12.

[4] *Ibid.,* no. 73, 11-14.

[5] Lucretius, *On the Nature of Things,* V.416-419.

[6] *Ibid.,* V.421-431.

[7] *Ibid.,* V.419-423.

[8] Comenius, *Naturall Philosophie Reformed by Divine Light,* 84.

[9] *Ibid.,* 36-37. Cf. Fludd, *Utriusque Cosmi Maioris scilicet et Minoris Metaphysica, Physica, atque Technica Historia,* II, 69-70; Collier, *Cosmogonies of Our Fathers,* 338-360 (see also Index), where an amazingly thorough and distinguished account may be found of sixteenth- and seventeenth-century opinion on the nature and creative function of primitive light. On the popularity of atomism in these centuries, see Harrison, *Harvard Studies and Notes in Philology and Literature,* XV (1933), 191-218, and *Harvard Studies in Classical Philology,* XLV (1934), 1-79.

[10] Reported by Aristotle, *De Caelo,* 303a.5-25.

[11] *On the Nature of Things,* II.1112-1116.

[12] See *Paradise Lost,* II, 889-907, and *supra,* 79.

[13] *On the Nature of Things,* V.449-475.

[14] *Ibid.,* V.499-500 *passim.*

[15] So Verity, *Milton: Paradise Lost,* 451.

[16] Cicero reports Zeno's views regarding natural substances as follows: "First, in dealing with the four recognized primary elements he did not add this fifth substance which his predecessors deemed to be the source of sensation and of intellect; for he laid it down that the natural substance that was the parent of all things . . . was itself fire." *Academica,* ed. and trans. H. Rackham, Loeb Classical Library (London, 1933), I.xi.39.

[17] See *A New English Dictionary, s.v.* ether 2, and quotations.

[18] Collier, 308, 352, 356, etc. Cf. George Hakewill, "The ancient *Fathers* and Doctours of the *Primitive Church,* for the most part following Plato, holde that it [the substance of the heavens] agrees with the *matter* of the *Elementary Bodies,* yet so as it is compounded of the finest flowre, and choisest delicacy of the *Elements.*" *An Apologie or Declaration of the Power and Providence of God in the Government of the World* (Oxford, 1630), 73. Thomas Vaughan agrees that "There is no fifth principle—no quintessence as Aristotle dreamed—but God Almighty." *The Works of Thomas Vaughan,* ed. A. E. Waite (London, 1919), 25.

19 *Naturall Philosophie*, 81.

20 *Ibid.*, 79.

21 The Sun's body is, of course, made of ether, and Satan sees every aspect of its glowing landscape informed with radiant light. But aside from the light, he is not sure whether the Sun's substance is metal or stone: if metal, part seemed gold, part clear silver; if stone, carbuncle, chrysolite, ruby, topaz, or the celebrated philosopher's stone vainly sought in earth. He seems finally convinced, however, that he has here discovered that pure quintessential elixir, the fabled alchemical substance sought by sublimation of common elements, which philosophers imagined capable of transmuting baser metals into gold. What wonder, then, that here "rivers run Potable Gold" (III, 591-607 *passim*). Cf. V, 415-426. On the alchemist's "divine quintessence," see Paracelsus, *The Hermetic and Alchemical Writings*, trans. Arthur Edward Waite (2 vols., London, 1894), I, 52.

22 From Grant McColley's excellent "The Astronomy of *Paradise Lost*," *Studies in Philology*, XXXIV (1937), 243.

23 Gomperz, *Greek Thinkers*, I, 337. On the atomic "membrane" of Leucippus, see Bailey, *The Greek Atomists and Epicurus*, 90 f., 95, 96 f., 99.

24 Seneca, *Questiones Naturales*, ed. and trans. into French, Paul Oltramare (Paris, 1929), VII.xiii.2. I am indebted for this reference to McColley, who remarks (243), "Had these atoms been the quintessence, the beliefs of Milton and of Artemidorus as to the formation and composition of the outer shell would be almost identical," and note, "One account is mechanistic; the other theistic."

25 *On the Nature of Things*, I.73.

26 *Ibid.*, V.465-472.

27 *Epicurus, The Extant Remains*, no. 88, 9.

28 *Ibid.*, no. 92, 9 ff. Lucretius agrees that "It may be too that all the sky remains at rest, while yet the shining constellations are borne on," V.517.

29 See Allan H. Gilbert, "The Outside Shell of Milton's World," *Studies in Philology*, XX (1923), 444-447, and *On the Composition of Paradise Lost* (Chapel Hill, 1947), 79-80.

30 Observe how admirably Harris Francis Fletcher represents the rabbinical sources and associations of this scene. *Milton's Rabbinical Readings*, 100-109.

31 *Ibid.*, 90 ff.

32 Gunkel, *Schöpfung und Chaos in Urzeit und Endzeit*, 17, 19. I use Walter Scott's translation of Gunkel's German into English. *Hermetica*, II, 126.

33 *Hermetica*, I, 115.

34 *Ibid.*, 147.

35 *Ibid.*, II, 123. Diogenes Laertius, *Lives of Eminent Philosophers*, VII. 130, 142.

36 *The History of the World*, ed. Oldys and Birch, in *The Works of Sir Walter Ralegh* (8 vols., London, 1929), II, 9.

37 *Naturall Philosophie*, 28.

38 See *infra*, 180-181.

39 Comenius, 11.

40 See Verity, 538.

41 From *Hermetica*, Libellvs III.1b-2b. Cf. a similar order of development in Libellvs I.8b,5b, of the same work: "The watery substance, having received the Word was fashioned into an ordered world, the elements being separated out from it; and from the elements came forth the brood of living creatures. Fire unmixed leapt forth from the watery substance, and rose up aloft; the fire was light and keen, and active. And therewith the air too, being light, followed the fire, and mounted up till it reached the fire, parting from earth and water; so that it seemed that the air was suspended from the fire. And the fire was encompassed by a mighty power, and was held fast, and stood firm. But earth and water remained in their own place . . . and this second Mind made out of fire and air seven Administrators [i.e., planets], who encompass with their orbits the world perceived by sense." This account has Neoplationic affinities, says Scott, *ibid.*, II, 31 ff.

42 For an excellent resume of the Stoic *diacosmesis* in relation to this passage, see *ibid.*, II, 123-126.

43 In the seventeenth century, says Collier (339), "Matter was generally conceived to be a chaos of particles."

44 See *ibid.*, 338-341, for an extensive survey of opinion. Cf. Du Bartas, *His Divine Weekes and Workes*, 12; and the Appendix.

45 Compare this with the modern physicist's concept of light: electric energy is converted into heat which causes molecules of various substances to vibrate with sufficient energy so that they radiate electromagnetic waves. These electromagnetic waves strike upon visual centers, and the resulting sensation is interpreted as light.

46 Comenius, 11, 12, 37, 81.

47 *Ibid.*, 80.

48 *Ibid.*, 86.

49 *Ibid.*, 88.

50 On the vague and conflicting opinions of seventeenth-century writers regarding the identity and nature of this "firmament," see Collier, 302-305, and on the mystery of "upper waters" and "lower waters," *ibid.*, 364-374.

51 "of elements / The grosser feeds the purer, earth the sea, / Earth and the sea feed air, and the air those fires / Ethereal, and as lowest first the moon" (V, 415-418). It is worthy of note that in *Paradise Lost* the term *ethereal* seems to be rather loosely used. But since all things are made of a common matter, we must remember the "ethereal" or "ethereal quintessence" may refer to any substance characterized by more or less rarity, refinement, or sublimation of the original elemental materials. For example, the bodies of angels are ethereal, and man may hope to purify his own body to that level (see *infra*, 171-176, *passim*); the floor of Heaven of Heavens is

an "ethereous mold" sublimated by Heaven's ray from the chaos below (VI, 473-481); heavenly trumpets, shields, light, and the throne of God are "ethereal" or "ethereal quintessence"; so are the stars, which move in a rarefied "ethereal air" or "ethereal sky."

52 On the location of planets and stars in the firmament, see Collier, 303-305.

53 For seventeenth-century support of this concept, see *ibid.*, 342 and n. 12.

54 See *infra*, Chapter 5. Cf. W. B. Hunter, "Milton and Thrice Great Hermes," *Journal of English and Germanic Philology*, XLV (1946), 327-336.

55 I have already shown how God, the Efficient Cause or First Mover, sends forth his creative power through a hierarchy of subordinate causes in the production of the World. *Supra*, 39-40.

56 We are not here concerned with the actuation of further life-forms from implanted *rationes seminales*, which constitutes activities of the last two days. But see *infra*, 177-182.

57 The substance of this chapter appeared first in *Anglia*, LXX (1952), 129-149.

CHAPTER FIVE

1 Marcus Tullius Cicero, *Somnium Scipionis*, ed. and trans. James A. Kleist (New York, 1915), no. 6, 29.

2 The Emperor Julian, *Hymn to King Helios*, 131C, ed. and trans. Wilmer Cave Wright, in *The Works of the Emperor Julian*, Loeb Classical Library (3 vols., London, 1913-1923), I, 355. Cf. *Hermetica*, I, 269, 273, 267, 348; III, 20.

3 See *infra*, Chapter VII, and *supra*, Chapter IV; *Shakespeare's Philosophical Patterns*, 32 ff.

4 For a full discussion of this ethereal quintessence and its location in the firmament of heaven, see *supra*, 110-111.

5 George Hakewill, *An Apologie or Declaration of the Power and Providence of God in the Government of the World* (Oxford, 1630), 74. Here Hakewill says that this "opinion is stiffely maintained by many great & learned Clarkes, both *Iewes*, and *Gentiles*, and *Christians*." For a full review of this question with a learned refutation, see Claudius Espencaeus, *De Coelorvm Animatione*, in *Opera Omnia* (Paris, 1619), 948-975.

6 William Gilbert (1540-1603), *The Loadstone and Magnetic Bodies*, trans. P. Fleury Mottelay (New York, 1893), 105-106.

7 *Ibid.*, 109.

8 *Ibid.*, 123.

9 *Ibid.*, 113.

10 *Ibid.*, 150.

11 *Ibid.*, 322, 333.

12 *Ibid.*, 334.

[13] *An Apologie or Declaration*, 73.

[14] Robert Boyle, *General History of the Air*, in *The Works of Robert Boyle* (6 vols., London, 1772), V, 640; quoted from W. B. Hunter, "The Seventeenth Century Doctrine of Plastic Nature," *Harvard Theological Review*, XLIII (1950), 205-206.

[15] *Ibid.*

[16] *The Loadstone and Magnetic Bodies*, 308-309.

[17] *Ibid.*, 110.

[18] *Ibid.*, 311.

[19] *An Apologie or Declaration*, 74. On this matter of the animated stars, Espence refers to the celebrated theologian, Ioannes Eckius, "qui positionem hanc ludicram prorsus & exoticam, execrabilem, & à fide exorbitantem esse censuit." *Ibid.*, 958.

[20] It is not by chance that Raphael closes his first account of creation with the line, "And earth self balanced on her center hung" (VII, 242). This business of the earth's being self-balanced on her magnetic center seems to imply the presence of an energic form.

[21] See *supra*, 99-100. Cf. Cicero, *Academica*, I.xi.39; Hakewill, 73; *The Works of Thomas Vaughan*, ed. A. E. Waite (London, 1919), 25; Comenius, *Naturall Philosophie Reformed by Divine Light*, 79.

[22] *Hermetica*, Libellvs XVI.9 (I, 269), and Scott's notes, II, 447-448. See also "All bodies are subject to change; but not all bodies are dissoluble." *Stobaei Hermetica*, Excerpt XI.2.(2), *ibid.*, I, 427.

[23] Cicero, *De Natura Deorum*, II.xxxiii.84. (Cf. *Hermetica*, II, 441).

[24] *De Natura Deorum*, II.xlvi.118; II.xxxiii.83.

[25] Diogenes Laertius, *Lives of Eminent Philosophers*, VII.144, on the authority of Posidonius.

[26] Cicero, *De Natura Deorum*, II.xv.40.

[27] Plutarch, *The Contradictions of the Stoics*, trans E. Smith, in *Plutarch's Morals* (5 vols., Boston, 1870), IV.xli.568. Cf. especially Ioannes ab Arnim, *Stoicorum Veterum Fragmenta* (3 vols., Leipzig, 1923), II, 196 ff.

[28] On the association of these several luminous stones by encyclopedists with the sun, see Kester Svendsen, "Milton and the Encyclopedias of Science," *Studies in Philology*, XXXIX (1942), 314-315. Cf. George Frederick Kunz, *The Magic of Jewels and Charms* (Philadelphia, 1915): luminous carbuncle, 378, chrysolite, one of "radiant luminaries," 287, ruby, "brilliant as a flame," 279; Kunz, *The Curious Lore of Precious Stones* (Philadelphia, 1913): chrysolite, gem of the sun, 347, luminosity of the ruby, 101-102, stones on the High-priest's breastplate, 275-302.

[29] John Read, *Prelude to Chemistry* (London, 1936), 102, explains in some detail the relationship between Sol, "sophic sulphur," or gold and Luna, "sophic mercury," or silver.

[30] Arnaldi de Villanova, *Rosarium Philosophorum*, I.x, in J. J. Manget's *Bibliotheca Chemica Curiosa* (2 vols., Geneva, 1702), I, 666. I am indebted to Dr. Edgar H. Duncan for the translation.

31 *Ibid.*, I.vii (Manget, I, 664-665). Translation quoted from E. H. Duncan, "Chaucer and 'Arnold of the Newe Toun'," *Modern Language Notes,* LXII (1942), 32.

32 Paracelsus, *The Hermetic and Alchemical Writings,* I, 65.

33 Read, 25.

34 Paracelsus, I, 249.

35 Read, 102.

36 Paracelsus, I, 65.

37 Thomas Norton, *The Ordinall of Alchimy,* Facsimile reproduction from *Theatrum Chemicum Britannicum* with an Introduction by E. J. Holmyard (Baltimore, 1931), 90.

38 *The Works of Geber,* Englished by Richard Russell, 1678, ed. with Introduction by E. J. Holmyard (London, 1928), 116.

39 *Ibid.*, 86.

40 John Read, 160-163, shows how alchemists levied upon classical mythology for names to conceal the "truths" of their doctrines and the mysteries of their operations. He mentions, among others, such symbolical figures as Artemis, Hercules, Sisyphus, Cadmus, Phoebus and Daphne, Jason, Medusa. But I can find nowhere in alchemical literature this Proteus used as a symbol for sulphur or anything else.

41 *The Works of Geber,* 59.

42 *Ibid.*, 60.

43 Paracelsus, I, 5 n.

44 *Ibid.*, 105.

45 *Ibid.*

46 *The Works of Geber,* 116-117 (see drawing of the aludels) and 230 (see drawing of the sublimatory furnace "after the manner of an *Alembeck* without a *Nose*").

47 *The Hermetic and Alchemical Writings,* II, 333.

48 *Ibid.*, I, 301.

49 *Ibid.*, II, 334.

50 *Ibid.*

51 Quoted from Read, 24.

52 *The Hermetic and Alchemical Writings,* I, 301.

53 *Ibid.*, II, 106, 130.

54 For a different interpretation of this passage, cf. W. B. Hunter, "Two Milton Notes," *Modern Language Review,* XLIV (1949), 89-90.

55 As Milton says, "Lucem sine lumine concipere animo non possumus; nec ideo lumen idem esse quod lucem, aut par dignitate arbitramur," *De Doctrina Christiana,* XV, 30. On the distinction between *lux* and *lumen* in classical writers, see Myrtle M. Cass, *The First Book of Jerome Cardan's De Subtilitate* (Williamsport, 1934), 145-146, n. 18.

56 Some in the seventeenth century, I have said elsewhere, have surmised that this Light is fire, or an attenuation of fire, or an efflux from the fiery element; some say it is a corporeal substance, and in no sense spiritual;

others conceive it to have been originally an invisible substance or power permeating all things and finally attaining visibility. Based on Collier, *Cosmogonies of Our Fathers*, 338-341.

[57] *Supra*, 108-109.

[58] See *supra*, 25-27.

[59] *Ibid.*

[60] I cannot therefore agree with such commentators as Sewell, Saurat, and others that holy light here addressed may be identified with the Son of God. For an adequate review of the controversy over the matter, see Kelley, *This Great Argument*, 91-93. He properly concludes that "the passage may not concern the Son at all but rather may be an invocation to light in the physical sense."

[61] E. T. Whittaker, Introduction to Sir Isaac Newton's *Opticks* (4th ed., New York, 1931), xiii. Cf. Descartes, *La Dioptrique*, Discourse I.3-4, published by Charles Adam and Paul Tannery in *Oeuvres de Descartes* (11 vols., Paris, 1897-1909), VI, 84.

[62] Quoted in *NED.*, s.v. pressure 2b.

[63] *Ibid.*, s.v. pression 2. Newton criticizes the theory as follows: "If Light consists only in Pression propagated without actual motion, it would not be able to agitate and heat Bodies which refract and reflect it. If it consisted in Motion propagated to all distances in an instant, it would require an infinite force every moment, in every shining Particle, to generate that Motion. And if it consisted in Pression or Motion, propagated in an instant or in time, it would bend into the Shadow." *Opticks*, 362.

[64] *An Apologie or Declaration*, 96.

[65] *General History of the Air*, 205.

[66] "Milton and the Thrice Great Hermes," *JEGPh.*, XLV (1946), 333 ff.

[67] Quoted from *ibid.*, 334.

[68] *Ibid.*, 333. I cannot agree, therefore, that when the human being dies, the soul returns to the sun. See *ibid.*, 335.

[69] See *supra*, 105, 111-112.

[70] The stars also, as we have seen, draw light from the Sun, augmenting their "small peculiar" by "tincture or reflection." Now "tincture" is an alchemical term; see my definition of it in Webster's *New International Dictionary*, s.v. tincture 4a: "An immaterial, quintessential, active principle believed capable, when infused, of causing material and spiritual transmutation." The arch-chemic Sun produces alchemical effects on the stars also.

[71] *Osiris*, XI (1954), 414. Dr. Duncan also speculates "that the beams from stars and planets are efficient instruments for the growth of precious underground productions in the universe of Paradise Lost." *Ibid.*, 413. "After all, metals and gems do grow." *Ibid.*, and n. 70.

[72] *Meteorlogica*, trans. E. W. Webster, Bk. III.6 (384a), in *The Works of Aristotle*, ed. W. D. Ross (11 vols., Oxford, 1908-1931), III.

[73] *Ibid.*

74 E. J. Holmyard, in the Introduction to his edition of *The Works of Geber,* xii. Quoted from Duncan, 392.

75 See Duncan's thorough review of the question, 392-400, *passim,* ending, "The burden of proof is still on those who would deny sulphur and mercury, or their sophic counterparts, as the proximate matter of metals. And such they are in the universe of Milton's *Paradise Lost.*"

76 Quoted from *NED., s.v.* temper 1.3.

77 *Mettallographia or An History of Mettals* (London, 1671), 72. Quoted from Duncan, 390.

78 Du Bartas, *His Divine Weekes and Workes,* 84.

79 *The Works of Geber,* xii-xiii; Duncan, 392.

80 *NED., s.v.* temper I.1.

81 Sir John Pettus, *Fodinae Ragales,* as quoted by Duncan, 411.

82 *The Hermetic and Alchemical Writings,* I, 22 n. Quoted from Duncan, 415.

CHAPTER SIX

1 I have given detailed discussion of concepts contained in this paragraph, *supra,* 24-26, 35, 43.

2 Gilbert, *On the Composition of Paradise Lost,* 97, n. 3. Cf. David Masson, *The Life of John Milton* (6 vols., Cambridge, Eng., 1859-1880), VI, 543, for a literal interpretation, and B. A. Wright, "Masson's Diagram of Milton's Spaces," *Review of English Studies,* XXI (1945), 42-44, for a rebuttal.

3 For a somewhat different interpretation of the passages about the road to Hell, as found in Book II and Book X, see Gilbert, 128-130.

4 The substance of this chapter appeared first in *Philological Quarterly,* XXIX (1950), 225-235.

CHAPTER SEVEN

1 See Robert Hunter West, *The Invisible World* (Athens, Georgia, 1939), 2, 27, 212, etc.; Cudworth, *The True Intellectual System of the Universe,* II, 256 ff.

2 I have belabored this question in *Shakespeare's Philosophical Patterns,* 175 ff. Cf. K. Svoboda, *La Demonologie de Michel Psellos* (Brno, 1927), 24-25; Robert Burton, *The Anatomy of Melancholy* (Oxford, 1621), part I, sect. ii, mem. i, subs. ii; Cudworth, II, 246-261; *The Commentaries of Hierocles, On the Golden Verses of Pythagoras,* in *The Life of Pythagoras, with his Symbols and Golden Verses, together with the Life of Hierocles, and his Commentaries upon the Verses,* trans. into French by M. Dacier, now done into English (London, 1707), 35, 36, 39; *Philosophical Writings*

of Henry More, ed. Flora Isabel Mackinnon (New York, 1925), 305-306; Marjorie H. Nicolson, "The Spirit World of Milton and More," *Studies in Philology*, XXII (1925), 433 ff.

[3] Origen, Preface to *De Principiis*, trans. Frederick Crombie, in *The Ante-Nicene Fathers* (10 vols., Buffalo, 1885-1897), IV, 241.

[4] Quoted from Cudworth, II, 257. This doctrine was approved by the seventh Oecumenical, or second Nicene council.

[5] Quoted, *ibid.*

[6]
                                        of elements
> The grosser feeds the purer, earth the sea,
> Earth and the sea feed air, the air those fires
> Ethereal, and as lowest first the moon . . .
> Nor doth the moon no nourishment exhale
> From her moist continent to higher orbs.
> The sun that light imparts to all, receives
> From all his alimental recompense
> In humid exhalations (V, 415-425).

[7] In the *De Doctrina Christiana*, XV, 41, 43, Milton admits a distinction between body, considered as a "mere senseless stock," and the spirit considered as an immaterial substance. "But," says he, "that the spirit of man should be separate from the body, so as to have a perfect and intelligent existence independently of it, is nowhere said in Scripture, and the doctrine is evidently at variance both with nature and reason."

[8] Cf. *ibid.*, 23: "For the original matter of which we speak, is not to be looked upon as an evil or trivial thing, but as intrinsically good, and the chief productive stock of every subsequent good. It was a substance, and derivable from no other source than from the fountain of every substance, though at first confused and formless, being afterwards adorned and digested into order by the hand of God." One must understand that this prime matter is ontologically prior to—not chronologically earlier than—that less remote material out of which God created the universe. He created, not out of matter alone, but out of matter adorned and endued with various forms; matter *per se* is only the seminary of every subsequent good. As Milton says (*A Fuller Institution of the Art of Logic*, in *Works*, XI, 51), "Matter is the cause from which a thing is"; but (59) "Form is the cause through which a thing is what it is."

[9] I have discussed Origen's opinion in this matter in "Arcite's Intellect," *JEGPh.*, XXIX (1930), 92.

[10] *De Principiis*, II.i. (IV, 270).

[11] *Ibid.*

[12] *Ibid.*, II.ii.2 (IV, 270). Professor Grant McColley has already adduced some of these passages from Origen in his admirable defense of Milton's orthodoxy, "Paradise Lost," *Harvard Theological Review*, XXXII (1939), 221.

[13] This is Solomon ibn Gebirol, variously called Avicebron, or Avencebrol

or Avicembrol, the first important Jewish philosopher in Spain, who wrote at Saragossa in the eleventh century.

14 Avencebrol, *Fons Vitae,* V.1. My general outline is based on C. R. S. Harris, *Duns Scotus* (2 vols., Oxford, 1927), I, 230-233; Maurice De Wulf, *History of Mediaeval Philosophy,* trans. E. C. Messenger (2 vols., New York, 1926), I, 228.

15 *Ibid.,* V.38: "To describe [God's] will is impossible; but it may be nearly described when one says that it is a divine virtue or power, creating matter and form and combining them, diffused from the highest to the lowest, . . . moving and disposing or ordering all things."

16 *Ibid.,* IV.10: et cum consideraueris omnes substantias, inuenies proprietates primae materiae et eius impressiones in eis; scilicet quod corpus est substantia sustinens formas multas diuersas, et praecipue natura et animae sensibiles, qua hae sunt imprimentes formas in corpore, et praecique anima rationalis et intelligentia, quia omnes formae sunt in eis.

17 *Ibid.,* V.22.

18 *Ibid.,* IV.14: Et propter hoc accidit quod una substantia est sapientior alia et perfectior, scilicet propter spissitudinem materiae et turbationem, non propter formam in se ipsa, quia scientia et cognitio ex forma est, non ex materia, quia forma est lumen purum, et materia e contrario, et quo fuerit materia subtilior et superior propter diffusionem luminis in illa, fiet ipsa substantia prudentior et perfectior, sicut intelligentia et anima; et e contrario [et] materia, quo magis descenderit, non fit spissa nisi propter elongationem luminis quod est infusum in illa et propter multiplicitatem partium eius.

19 *Summa Theologica,* I.L.2c. St. Thomas, who believes with Aristotle in abstract, separable spiritual substances, of course disagrees violently with Avencebrol.

20 See Harris, I, 154; De Wulf, I, 346-347.

21 See De Wulf, I, 365; Harris, I, 164. Neither Alexander nor St. Bonaventura acknowledges dependence upon Avencebrol. As Professor McColley shows (221), St. Bonaventura bases his conception of a universal and perhaps homogeneous matter in all things upon a passage from the pseudo-Augustinian *De Mirabilibus Sacrae Scripturae* (J. P. Migne, *Patrologiae Cursus Completus, Latina* (221 vols., Paris, 1844-1864), XXXV, 2151).

22 Harris, II, 81-82.

23 *Ibid.,* 83-84.

24 *De Rerum Principio,* q. viii, art. 4, n. 30; quoted from Harris, II, 84, n. 2.

25 Dun's symbol of the tree offers a closer parallel to Milton's, it seems to me, than that adduced by Denis Saurat (*Milton: Man and Thinker,* 305-306) from Robert Fludd. A reading of Fludd shows that his image of the tree is used merely to illustrate the physics of the cosmos, where the four elements are sublimated to the greatest degree of "spiritual" purity in the Sun in contrast with the grossness of the Earth. See Fludd, *Utriusque*

Cosmi, Maioris scilicet et Minoris Metaphysica, Physica atque Technica Historia, 137, where the passage occurs in the discussion De Solis, ortu & origine, etc.

26 *Commentaries,* 363-365.

27 *Ibid.,* 367. Cudworth (II, 218-228) supports this concept of the nature and function of the luciform body by quotations from Philoponus, Proclus, Psellus, Suidas and others. Cf. *Hermetica,* II, 263-265, where Scott traces the idea back through Iamblichus who "knew of certain Platonists who held that the soul, when not incorporated in an earthy body, is at all times incorporated in a material body of finer substance"—a concept adopted by Origen—to Heraclides. Henry Cornelius Agrippa (*Three Books of Occult Philosophy,* trans. F. F. (London, 1651), III.xxxvii.465) seems to be in the same tradition when he says: "The soul of man is a certain divine Light, created after the image of the word . . . ; therefore mans soul being such, according to the opinion of the *Platonists,* immediately proceeding from God, is joined by competent means to this grosser body; whence first of all in its descent, it is involved in a Celestiall . . . body, which they call the celestiall vehicle of the soul, others the chariot of the soul: Through this middle thing . . . it is first infused in the middle part of the heart . . . and from thence it is diffused through all the parts and members of his body, when it joyneth his chariot to the naturall heat."

28 *Commentaries,* 365-371.

29 Quoted from Cudworth, II, 229.

30 *Three Books of Occult Philosophy,* III.xliii.492. This elevation of the gross material body into higher realms is made possible because, as Agrippa says (I.viii.22), the four elements are found in all created things: "That Elements therefore are to be found every where, and in all things after their manner, no man can deny: First in those inferior bodies feculent, and gross, and in Celestials more pure and clear; but in supercelestials living, and in all respects blessed."

31 *The Immortality of the Soul,* I.xi, in *Philosophical Writings,* 98-99.

32 *Ibid.,* II.xv (153-155).

33 *The True Intellectual System,* II, 237.

34 George Rust, *A Letter of Resolution concerning Origen and the Chief of His Opinions,* 1661, ed. Marjorie Hope Nicolson, for the Facsimile Text Society (New York, 1933).

35 *Ibid.,* 8, etc.

36 *Ibid.,* 46-47.

37 *Ibid.*

38 *Ibid.,* 53.

39 *Ibid.,* 109-111.

40 *Ibid.,* 115-117.

41 *Logic,* XI, 59.

42 *Ibid.,* 51, 61.

43 *Milton: Man and Thinker,* 305.

44 Quoted from A. W. Verity, *Paradise Lost,* 494.

45 *Logic*, XI, 51.

46 I have already discussed the efflux of primary matter from the spiritual Being of God, *supra*, 33-34.

47 Professor Harris Francis Fletcher, in his excellent *Milton's Rabbinical Readings*, 122 ff., draws an illuminating distinction between the Act of Creation, which is immediate, and the process of the working out of creation through six days.

48 I have discussed at length this problem of Augustinian exemplarism in my *Shakespeare's Philosophical Patterns*, 32 ff. Milton, it seems to me, is here following Augustine or the Augustinian tradition in his representation of the impregnation of matter by the Spirit of God.

49 For different interpretations of God's "withdrawal," see Saurat, 286 ff., and Taylor, *Milton's Use of Du Bartas*, 42.

50 We must not forget that "soul" in this sense refers to the whole living creature composed of matter and form, matter instinct with the breath of life, and, in man, matter or body intimately blended with the rational soul or spirit. See again *De Doctrina Christiana*, XV, 41, 43. Here we are interested only in the origins of the rational soul.

51 As early as *Comus* (459-463) Milton toys with this idea, but he has not yet incorporated it into a philosophical system. His description (*Comus*, 465-469) of the soul's defilement by acts of sin until it loses "The divine property of her first being" smacks of the Neoplatonic conception of the pre-existent soul's fall through folly into the defiling body, though he is speaking merely of what may happen to the soul in this life.

52 For some different interpretations of the phrase *power of matter*, see William B. Hunter, "Milton's Materialistic Life Principle," *JEGPh.*, XLV (1946), 68 ff. and "Milton's Power of Matter," *Journal of the History of Ideas*, XIII (1952), 551-562.

53 The substance of this chapter appeared first in *Stanford Studies in Language and Literature*, ed. Hardin Craig (Stanford, California, 1941), 173-206.

APPENDIX

1 See Professor Fletcher's excellent *Milton's Rabbinical Readings*.

2 See *supra*, Chapters II and VII.

3 Saurat, *Milton: Man and Thinker*, 281 ff.

4 *The Zohar*, trans. Harry Sperling and Maurice Simon. See especially Simon's exposition, I, 379-380.

5 *Ibid.*, I, 380 ff.; II, 398. Parenthetical references in the text are to this edition.

6 See the table showing correspondence of the Grades with the cabbalistic Sefiroth, *ibid.*, I, 385.

7 Maurice Simon, *ibid.*, 381.

8 *Ibid.*, II, 398.

[9] *Ibid.*, I, 381.

[10] Simon, *ibid.*, 382.

[11] "And Diodorus the Eretrian and Aristoxenus the musician assert that Pythagoras came to Zaratas (Zoroaster) the Chaldean, and that he explained to him that there are two original causes of things, father and mother, and that the father is light, but the mother darkness." Hyppolytus, *The Refutation of all Heresies*, I.II, in *The Ante-Nicene Fathers*, V, 12.

[12] I John, 1:5.

[13] For example, see Alain de Lille, *Anticlaudian*, trans. William Hafner Cornog (Philadelphia, 1935), 106; Marsilio Ficino, *Commentary on Plato's Symposium*, trans. Sears Reynolds Jayne (Columbia, Missouri, 1944), 129; Du Bartas, *His Divine Weekes and Workes*, 2.

[14] I Timothy, 6:16.

[15] *Hermetica*, I, 115.

[16] Ginsburg, *The Kabbalah*, 96.

[17] So in the *vohar*, "Then the source of all lights shone forth and opened the gate of the East, for thence light issues" (I, 130, 34b); "Thus *Yod*, symbolic of the east, is the starting-point of light" (V, 168, 118b).

WALTER CLYDE CURRY, the author of this book, re-tired from the headship of the English department at Vanderbilt University in 1955, after having served the university for forty years. A native of South Carolina, he is a graduate of Wofford College. He holds M.A. and Ph.D. degrees from Stanford University. His previous books include *Chaucer and the Mediaeval Sciences* and *Shakespeare's Philosophical Patterns.*

MILTON'S ONTOLOGY, COSMOGONY, AND PHYSICS was composed and printed at the University of Kentucky. It is set in Linotype Caledonia, with headings in ATF Garamond. The book is printed on Warren's Olde Style antique wove paper and bound by the C. J. Krehbiel Company in Holliston's Roxite cloth.